NETWORK TESTING UNVEILED

The Ultimate Beginners Guide to Master Network Testing

Srinivasa Chary Musalogu

INDIA • SINGAPORE • MALAYSIA

Copyright © Srinivasa Chary Musalogu
All Rights Reserved.

This book has been self-published with all reasonable efforts taken to make the material error-free by the author. No part of this book shall be used, reproduced in any manner whatsoever without written permission from the author, except in the case of brief quotations embodied in critical articles and reviews.

The Author of this book is solely responsible and liable for its content including but not limited to the views, representations, descriptions, statements, information, opinions and references ["Content"]. The Content of this book shall not constitute or be construed or deemed to reflect the opinion or expression of the Publisher or Editor. Neither the Publisher nor Editor endorse or approve the Content of this book or guarantee the reliability, accuracy or completeness of the Content published herein and do not make any representations or warranties of any kind, express or implied, including but not limited to the implied warranties of merchantability, fitness for a particular purpose. The Publisher and Editor shall not be liable whatsoever for any errors, omissions, whether such errors or omissions result from negligence, accident, or any other cause or claims for loss or damages of any kind, including without limitation, indirect or consequential loss or damage arising out of use, inability to use, or about the reliability, accuracy or sufficiency of the information contained in this book.

Made with ♥ on the Notion Press Platform
www.notionpress.com

CONTENTS

About the Book......7
About the Author......9
Acknowledgements......11

1. Introduction......13
   1.1. Overview of Network Testing......13
   1.2. Importance in IT Infrastructure......14
   1.3. Goals and Objectives of the Book......15

2. Fundamentals of Network Testing......16
   2.1. Understanding Networks......16
   2.2. Types of Networks:......16
   2.3. Protocols and Communication Basics......20
   2.4. Packet level knowledge required......20
   2.5. Essential routing protocols......22
   2.6. Difference Between Functional Testing and Non-functional Testing......23

3. Types of Network Testing......25
   3.1. What is Functional Testing......25
   3.2. What is Performance Testing......27
   3.3. What is Security Testing......29
   3.4. What is Compatibility Testing......32
   3.5. What is Stress Testing......34

4. Test Planning and Strategy......37
   4.1. Defining Objectives and Scope......37
   4.2. Identifying Key Components......38

- 4.3. Developing Test Cases 40
- 4.4. Creating Test Scenarios 45

5. Test Tools and Technologies 49
   - 5.1. Overview of Network Testing Tools 49
   - 5.2. Popular Testing Frameworks 51
   - 5.3. Automation in Network Testing 53
   - 5.4. Virtualization and Emulation 55

6. Functional Testing 58
   - 6.1. Verifying Network Services 58
   - 6.2. Validating Connectivity 59
   - 6.3. Assessing Data Integrity 61

7. Performance Testing 65
   - 7.1. Bandwidth Testing 65
   - 7.2. Latency and Packet Loss Analysis 67
   - 7.3. Scalability Testing 68
   - 7.4. Throughput and Capacity Planning 70

8. Security Testing 74
   - 8.1. Vulnerability Assessment 74
   - 8.2. Penetration Testing 76
   - 8.3. Firewall and Intrusion Detection System Testing 78
   - 8.4. SSL/TLS Testing 80

9. Compatibility Testing 84
   - 9.1. Device and Platform Compatibility 84
   - 9.2. Interoperability Testing 86
   - 9.3. Browser Compatibility 89

10. Stress Testing 93
    - 10.1. Overload and Stability Testing 93
    - 10.3. Failover and Recovery Testing 97

11. Reporting and Documentation 101
    11.1. Importance of Comprehensive Reporting 101
    11.2. Documenting Test Results 103
    11.3. Communicating Findings to Stakeholders 105

12. Real-world Case Studies 111
    12.1. Success Stories 111
    12.2. Challenges Faced and Overcome 113
    12.3. Lessons Learned 115

13. Future Trends in Network Testing 119
    13.1. Emerging Technologies in Network Testing 119
    13.2. Evolving Testing Practices 121
    13.3. The Role of AI in Network Testing 123

14. Best Practices and Tips 125
    14.1. Efficient Test Planning 125
    14.2. Test Execution Strategies 126
    14.3. Continuous Improvement in Testing Processes 128

15. Conclusion 131
    15.1. Summary of Key Takeaways 131
    15.2. Encouragement for Continuous Learning 133

Appendix *135*
Glossary of Terms: *135*
Additional Resources: *135*

ABOUT THE BOOK

This comprehensive guide is tailored for professionals aspiring to forge a successful career in Network testing, whether in product development or IT companies involved in product deployment. Having scoured the internet in search of exhaustive resources on Network testing, I recognized a glaring gap in the available literature. Despite finding ample material on Software testing, there was a notable absence of dedicated resources focusing solely on Network testing—a void that inspired me to embark on this endeavor.

Drawing from my extensive 26+ years of experience in the field, I have meticulously compiled all-encompassing knowledge on Network testing within these pages. Leveraging insights gained from industry research into prevailing Network testing frameworks and tools utilized by leading Product and IT companies, this book equips readers with fundamental information essential for navigating the intricacies of Network testing.

Covering everything from the definition of key testing terms to the utilization of frameworks, tools, automation, and emerging testing trends, this book serves as a definitive resource for Network testing engineers seeking to excel in their careers. With clarity and conciseness as guiding principles, I have endeavored to encapsulate maximum pertinent information to empower readers on their journey toward mastery in Network testing.

ABOUT THE AUTHOR

Srinivasa Chary Musalogu is a seasoned expert in the field of Networking technology, boasting over 26 years of comprehensive experience in the IT industry. Throughout his distinguished career, he has assumed diverse roles including Network Engineer, Systems Engineer, Solution Architect, and Network Testing Lead, among others. He has contributed his expertise to renowned companies such as TATA, Reliance, Wipro, and Google.

With extensive international exposure, Srinivasa has had the privilege of engaging with clients across various countries including England, Finland, the Netherlands, Italy, France, Belgium, Switzerland, USA, Canada, the Middle East, Singapore, Japan, China, Thailand, and more. Notably, he has played a pivotal role in the establishment of numerous Data Centers worldwide, while consistently achieving client Network certifications.

In addition to his professional achievements, Srinivasa is deeply committed to coaching and mentoring professionals in his field, guiding them in their career growth and development. He finds immense fulfillment in sharing his knowledge and expertise, empowering others to excel in their respective roles and aspirations.

Beyond his professional pursuits, Srinivasa possesses a passion for travel, eagerly immersing himself in diverse cultures and culinary experiences across the globe.

ACKNOWLEDGEMENTS

First and foremost, I would like to extend my deepest gratitude to my mentor and coach, Dr. Manjunath, for his unwavering support and guidance. Your encouragement, wisdom, and belief in my potential have been the driving force behind the creation of this book. You set ambitious targets and pushed me to reach beyond my limits, and for that, I will always be grateful.

To my wonderful family, my heartfelt thanks go to my wife, Santhoshi, whose love and support have been my strength throughout this journey. To my mother, Laxmi, thank you for your endless encouragement and belief in my abilities. To my children, Varun and Rishikesh, you inspire me every day. Special thanks to Rishikesh for assisting me with the diagrams and ensuring everything was organized perfectly—your help made a significant impact on the completion of this book.

I also want to extend my appreciation to my publisher, Notion Press Media Private Limited, for their belief in this project and for making the publishing process a smooth and rewarding experience.

This book is a product of all your support, and I am deeply thankful.

CHAPTER 01
INTRODUCTION

1.1. Overview of Network Testing

Network testing is an essential practice in the field of information technology (IT), aimed at ensuring the reliability, performance, and security of computer networks. As the backbone of modern digital infrastructure, networks facilitate communication, data transfer, and access to resources across various devices and locations. However, the complexity and criticality of networks also introduce vulnerabilities and challenges that necessitate rigorous testing methodologies.

At its core, network testing involves the systematic examination and evaluation of network components, protocols, and configurations to identify weaknesses, optimize performance, and mitigate risks. It encompasses a diverse range of testing types, including functional, performance, security, compatibility, and stress testing, each focusing on different aspects of network behavior and functionality.

Functional testing validates the correct operation of network services and features, ensuring that devices can communicate effectively and services are accessible to users.

Performance testing assesses the network's capacity, throughput, and responsiveness under various conditions, helping to identify bottlenecks and optimize resource utilization.

Security testing is crucial for identifying vulnerabilities and ensuring that network infrastructure is resilient against cyber threats. This includes vulnerability assessment, penetration testing, and validation of security mechanisms such as firewalls and encryption protocols.

Compatibility testing ensures seamless integration and interoperability of network components, devices, and applications, minimizing compatibility issues that could disrupt operations or compromise performance.

Stress testing evaluates the network's resilience and stability under extreme conditions, such as heavy traffic loads or hardware failures, to identify potential points of failure and implement appropriate failover mechanisms.

Effective network testing requires careful planning, execution, and documentation to achieve meaningful results and facilitate informed decision-making. It involves the use of specialized tools and technologies for network discovery, traffic analysis, protocol validation, and security assessment. Automation and virtualization play increasingly important roles in streamlining testing processes and enabling scalability and repeatability.

In today's rapidly evolving IT landscape, network testing is more critical than ever to ensure the integrity, availability, and security of digital infrastructure. By adopting a comprehensive and proactive approach to network testing, organizations can mitigate risks, optimize performance, and enhance the resilience of their networks to meet the demands of modern business environments.

1.2. Importance in IT Infrastructure

Network testing holds a paramount position within the realm of IT infrastructure, serving as the cornerstone for ensuring the reliability, performance, and security of interconnected systems. In the modern digital landscape, where organizations rely heavily on technology to drive their operations, the importance of robust and resilient networks cannot be overstated.

At the heart of every organization's IT infrastructure lies a complex network of interconnected devices, servers, applications, and data repositories. This network facilitates communication, data transfer, and access to resources across various locations, enabling seamless collaboration and productivity. However, with this interconnectedness comes inherent risks and vulnerabilities that can pose significant threats to organizational operations and data security.

Network failures, performance bottlenecks, security breaches, and compatibility issues can all have far-reaching consequences, ranging from disruption of services and loss of productivity to financial losses and reputational damage. In today's hyper-connected world, where cyber threats are constantly evolving and the volume of data exchanged over networks continues to soar, the stakes of network reliability and security have never been higher.

This is where network testing emerges as a critical tool in the arsenal of IT professionals. By subjecting network infrastructure to rigorous testing methodologies, organizations can identify weaknesses, uncover vulnerabilities, and proactively address potential points of failure before they escalate into a full-blown crisis. Whether it's validating the functionality of network services, assessing performance under varying loads, or fortifying defenses against cyber threats, network testing provides invaluable insights and assurance.

Moreover, network testing plays a pivotal role in ensuring compliance with regulatory requirements and industry standards governing data security and privacy. By demonstrating adherence to best practices and regulatory mandates through comprehensive testing and documentation, organizations can instill confidence among stakeholders and safeguard sensitive information from unauthorized access or disclosure.

In essence, network testing is not just a reactive measure to detect and remediate issues as they arise; it is a proactive strategy to fortify the foundations of IT infrastructure and enhance resilience in the face of evolving threats and challenges. By investing in robust network testing practices, organizations can mitigate risks, optimize performance, and uphold the integrity and availability of their critical systems, thereby enabling innovation, growth, and competitive advantage in today's digital economy.

1.3. Goals and Objectives of the Book

The primary goal of "**Network Testing Unveiled: The Ultimate Beginners Guide to Mastering Network Testing**" is to provide IT professionals, network test engineers, network engineers, system administrators, and aspiring network enthusiasts with a comprehensive and practical resource to master the art and science of network testing.

This book aims to demystify the complex landscape of network testing by offering clear explanations, real-world examples, and hands-on guidance on various testing methodologies, tools, and best practices. Whether you are a seasoned network testing expert seeking to deepen your knowledge or a novice embarking on a journey to understand the fundamentals of network testing, this book is designed to cater to diverse skill levels and backgrounds.

The objectives of the book are multifaceted:

Comprehensive Coverage: The book strives to cover a wide range of topics related to network testing, including functional testing, performance testing, security testing, compatibility testing, and stress testing. By providing a holistic view of network testing, readers can develop a thorough understanding of its various dimensions and applications.

Practical Guidance: In addition to theoretical concepts, the book offers practical guidance on planning, executing, and documenting network tests. Through step-by-step instructions, real-world case studies, and tips from industry experts, readers can gain actionable insights and hands-on experience to apply in their own professional environments.

Empowerment Through Knowledge: By equipping readers with the knowledge and skills needed to effectively test and optimize network infrastructure, the book aims to empower them to overcome challenges, mitigate risks, and enhance the reliability, performance, and security of their networks. Whether it's identifying and addressing vulnerabilities, optimizing bandwidth utilization, or ensuring compatibility across devices and platforms, readers will emerge with the confidence and expertise to tackle diverse network testing scenarios.

Future Readiness: The book also explores emerging trends and technologies in network testing, such as automation, virtualization, and the role of artificial intelligence. By staying abreast of future trends and innovations, readers can future-proof their skills and adapt to the evolving demands of the IT landscape.

In essence, "**Network Testing Unveiled**" is not just a book; it's a roadmap to mastery, guiding readers on a journey to unlock the full potential of network testing and harness its transformative power in today's interconnected world.

FUNDAMENTALS OF NETWORK TESTING

CHAPTER 02

2.1. Understanding Networks

To embark on the journey of mastering network testing, it's essential to first establish a solid understanding of networks themselves. Networks form the backbone of modern communication, facilitating the exchange of data and enabling connectivity between devices across various geographical locations. At its core, a network is a collection of interconnected devices, such as computers, servers, routers, Firewalls, Load Balancers, Cache engines, switches etc.., configured to share resources and information.

2.2. Types of Networks:

Networks can be classified into different types based on their geographical scope and architecture:

Local Area Network (LAN): A LAN typically covers a small geographic area, such as an office building or a campus. It allows devices within the network to communicate with each other directly and efficiently.

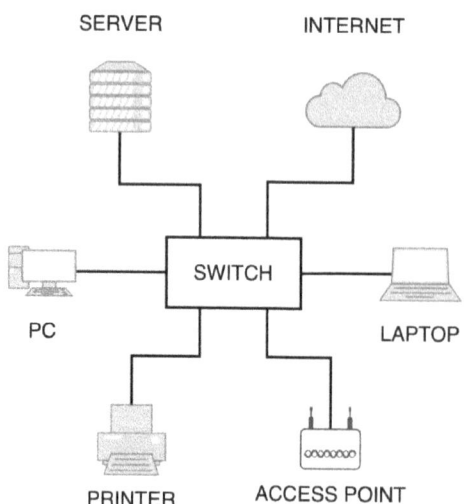

Fig-2.2.1: Local Area Network (LAN)

Wide Area Network (WAN): A WAN spans a larger geographic area, often connecting multiple LANs across different locations. It relies on long-distance communication technologies, such as leased lines or satellite links, to interconnect remote sites.

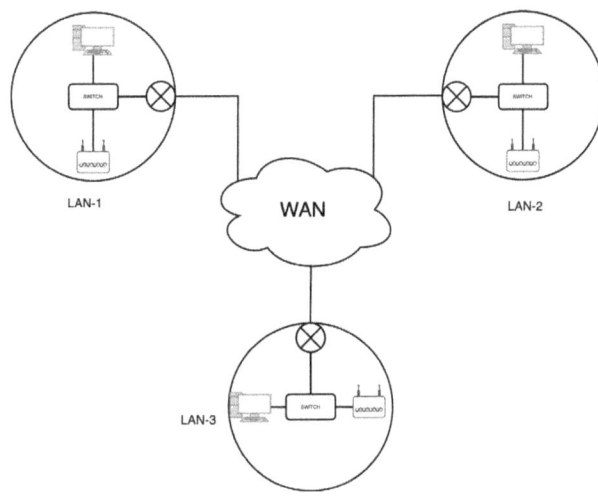

Fig-2.2.2: Wide Area Network (WAN)

Metropolitan Area Network (MAN): MANs bridge the gap between LANs and WANs, covering a larger geographic area than a LAN but smaller than a WAN. They are often used to interconnect multiple LANs within a city or metropolitan area.

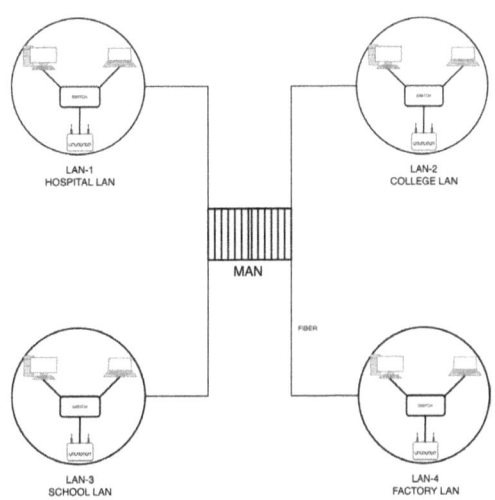

Fig-2.2.3: Metropolitan Area Network (MAN)

Network testing Topologies:

Network testing topologies vary based on the objectives of the testing and the resources available. Here are three common network testing topologies:

1. Hardware Topologies:

Single Device: This topology involves testing a single networking device, such as a router, switch, or firewall, in isolation. It allows for detailed testing of the device's functionality, performance, and security features.

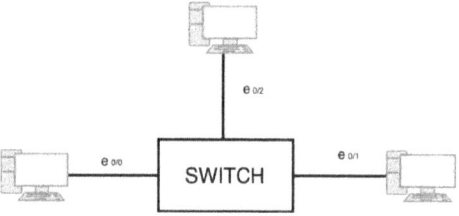

Fig-2.2.4: Single Device

Triangle Topology: In a triangle topology, three networking devices are interconnected to form a triangle. This topology enables testing of basic network connectivity, routing protocols, and failover mechanisms.

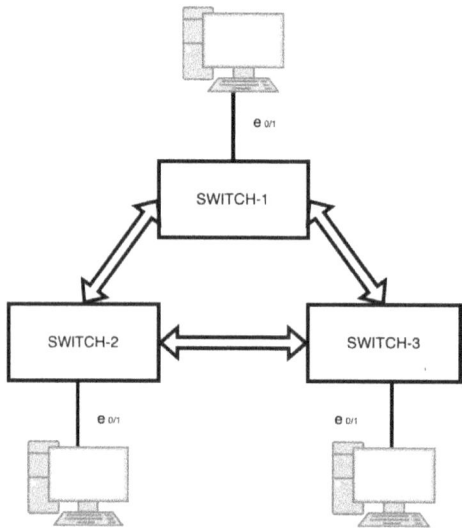

Fig-2.2.5: Triangle Topology

Four Devices Topology: This topology extends the triangle topology by adding a fourth networking device. It allows for more complex testing scenarios, such as multi-path routing, redundancy, and load balancing.

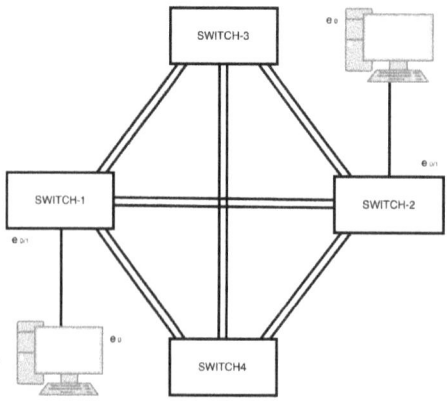

Fig-2.2.6: Four Devices Topology

2. Hybrid Topologies:

Hardware and Simulation Devices: In hybrid topologies, a combination of physical networking devices and virtual or simulated devices are used. For example, physical routers and switches may be connected to a network simulator or emulator, allowing for a mix of real-world and simulated testing scenarios. This approach provides flexibility and scalability while minimizing costs.

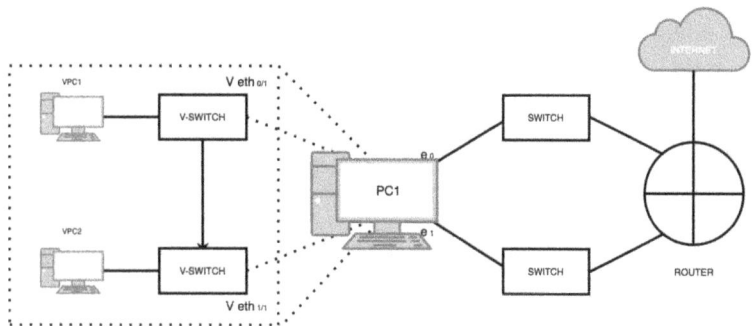

Fig-2.2.7: Hardware and Simulation Devices

3. Fully Simulated (Software) Topologies:

Virtualized Environment: In fully simulated topologies, all networking devices are virtualized using software-based solutions. Virtual routers, switches, firewalls, and other network components are created and interconnected within a virtualized environment. Tools such as GNS3, Cisco VIRL, or EVE-NG are commonly used to simulate complex network topologies for testing purposes. This approach offers complete control over the network environment and allows for testing of a wide range of scenarios without the need for physical hardware.

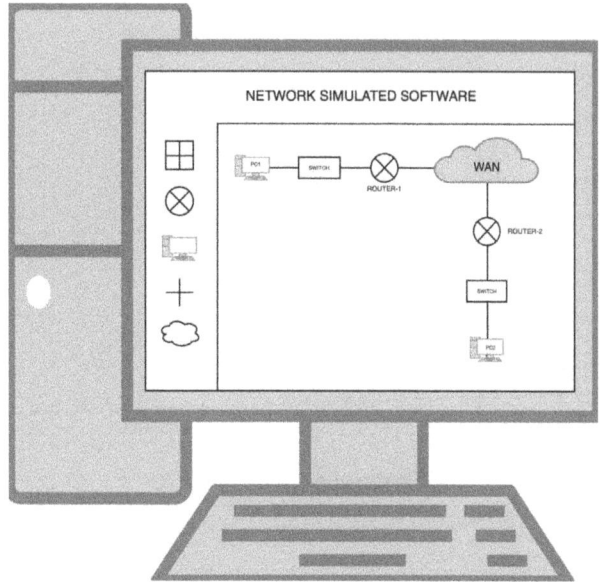

Fig-2.2.8: Virtualized Environment

Each of these network testing topologies has its advantages and limitations, and the choice depends on factors such as the scope of testing, available resources, budget constraints, and specific requirements of the testing environment. By selecting the appropriate topology and leveraging the right tools and technologies, network engineers can effectively validate and optimize the performance, reliability, and security of their network infrastructures.

2.3. Protocols and Communication Basics

Networks rely on protocols to govern communication between devices and ensure data exchange occurs seamlessly. Protocols define rules and conventions for formatting, transmitting, and receiving data packets. Common network protocols include:

TCP/IP (Transmission Control Protocol/Internet Protocol): The foundational protocol suite of the internet, responsible for routing data packets between devices and ensuring reliable communication.

Ethernet: A widely used protocol for local area networks, defining standards for data transmission over wired connections.

Wi-Fi (IEEE 802.11): A set of standards for wireless communication, enabling devices to connect to a network without the need for physical cables.

HTTP (Hypertext Transfer Protocol): The protocol used for transferring web pages and other resources on the World Wide Web.

By understanding the fundamental concepts of networks, including their types, topologies, and protocols, aspiring network testers lay a solid groundwork for comprehending the intricacies of network testing. A clear grasp of these concepts enables testers to navigate through the complexities of network infrastructure, identify potential areas of concern, and devise effective testing strategies to ensure the reliability and performance of networks in various environments.

2.4. Packet level knowledge required

In the realm of network testing, a fundamental understanding of packet-level communication is indispensable. Networks transmit data in the form of packets, discrete units of information that traverse the network infrastructure from source to destination. To effectively analyze, troubleshoot, and optimize network performance, testing engineers must possess in-depth knowledge of various packet types, including Ethernet, TCP, UDP, and others.

Ethernet Packets:

Ethernet is the most widely used networking technology for local area networks (LANs). Ethernet packets, also known as frames, encapsulate data for transmission over Ethernet networks. Each Ethernet frame consists of a header containing source and destination MAC addresses, payload data, and a trailer with error-checking information. Understanding Ethernet frames is crucial for analyzing network traffic, identifying sources of congestion or errors, and ensuring the efficient transmission of data within LAN environments.

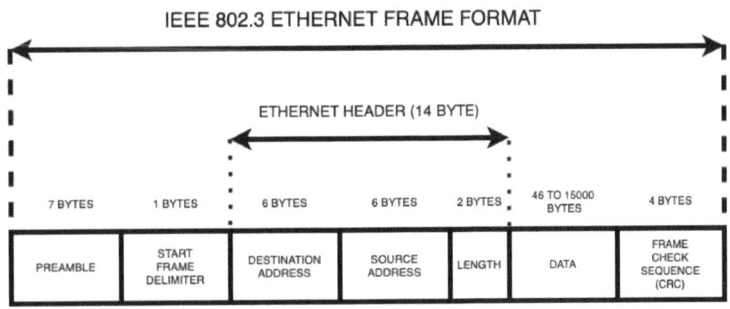

Fig-2.4.1: Ethernet Packets

TCP (Transmission Control Protocol) Packets:

TCP is a connection-oriented protocol that facilitates reliable and ordered data delivery between devices on a network. TCP packets, encapsulated within IP packets, manage the establishment, maintenance, and termination of connections, as well as flow control and error recovery mechanisms. Each TCP packet contains header fields such as source and destination ports, sequence numbers, acknowledgment numbers, and checksums. Testing engineers must be familiar with TCP packet structures and behaviors to diagnose network performance issues, troubleshoot connectivity problems, and optimize TCP-based applications.

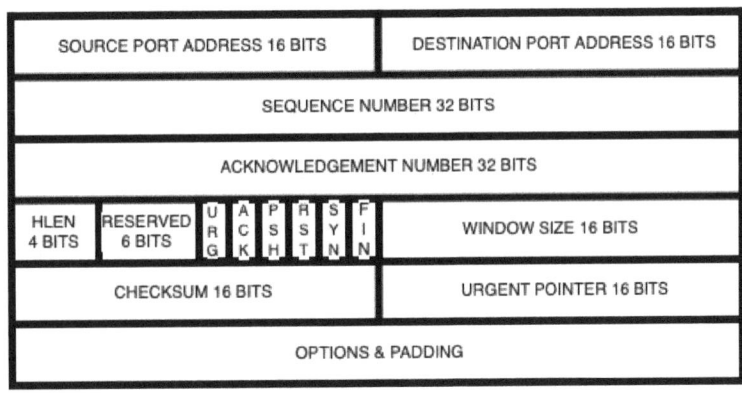

Fig-2.4.2: TCP (Transmission Control Protocol) Packets

UDP (User Datagram Protocol) Packets:

UDP is a connectionless protocol that provides a lightweight, best-effort method of data transmission across IP networks. UDP packets are simpler than TCP packets, containing minimal header information, including source and destination ports and checksums. Unlike TCP, UDP does not provide reliability, flow control, or error recovery mechanisms, making it suitable for real-time and latency-sensitive applications where occasional packet loss or out-of-order delivery is acceptable. Understanding UDP packet characteristics is essential for testing engineers involved in applications such as VoIP, video streaming, and online gaming.

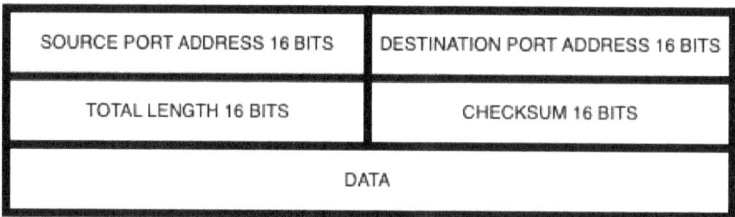

Fig-2.4.2: UDP Packets

In conclusion, a comprehensive understanding of packet-level communication, including Ethernet, TCP, UDP, and other protocols, is essential for network testing engineers. Mastery of packet analysis techniques enables engineers to diagnose network issues, optimize performance, and ensure the reliable delivery of data across diverse network environments. By acquiring packet-level knowledge, testing engineers empower themselves to tackle complex networking challenges with confidence and expertise.

2.5. Essential routing protocols

Routing protocols are essential in networking for determining the best paths for data to travel within a network. Here are some of the most commonly used routing protocols in the networking industry:

Routing Information Protocol (RIP): RIP is one of the oldest routing protocols. It operates based on the hop count metric, where the number of routers a packet must traverse to reach its destination is counted. RIP versions include RIP v1 and RIP v2.

Open Shortest Path First (OSPF): OSPF is a link-state routing protocol that calculates the shortest path to a destination based on the cost of links. It uses Dijkstra's algorithm to determine the shortest path tree. OSPF is widely used in large enterprise networks and internet service provider (ISP) networks.

Border Gateway Protocol (BGP): BGP is the routing protocol used on the internet to exchange routing information between different autonomous systems (ASes). Unlike interior gateway protocols (IGPs) such as OSPF and RIP, BGP is an exterior gateway protocol (EGP) that operates between different autonomous systems.

Interior Gateway Routing Protocol (IGRP): IGRP is a Cisco proprietary distance-vector routing protocol. It is similar to RIP but offers improvements in terms of convergence time and scalability. IGRP uses a composite metric based on bandwidth and delay.

Enhanced Interior Gateway Routing Protocol (EIGRP): EIGRP is another Cisco proprietary routing protocol that combines features of both distance-vector and link-state routing protocols. It uses the Diffusing Update Algorithm (DUAL) to calculate the shortest path to a destination based on bandwidth, delay, reliability, and load.

Intermediate System-to-Intermediate System (IS-IS): IS-IS is a link-state routing protocol that is commonly used in large service provider networks. It is similar to OSPF but is more scalable and efficient in certain scenarios.

Routing Information Protocol next generation (RIPng): RIPng is an extension of RIP designed to support IPv6 networks. It operates similarly to RIP but is adapted for IPv6 addressing and routing.

Multi-Protocol Label Switching (MPLS): MPLS is not a routing protocol per se but a technique used to speed up and shape network traffic flows. It allows routers to make forwarding decisions based on labels rather than IP addresses, improving performance and flexibility.

These are just a few examples of the routing protocols used in the networking industry. The choice of routing protocol depends on factors such as network size, topology, traffic patterns, and organizational requirements.

2.6. Difference Between Functional Testing and Non-functional Testing

In the context of networking devices testing, understanding the difference between functional testing and non-functional testing is crucial for ensuring comprehensive evaluation and validation of network infrastructures. Here's a breakdown of each:

Functional Testing:

Functional testing evaluates the specific functions and features of networking devices to ensure they operate as intended and meet the functional requirements outlined for them. In the context of networking devices testing, functional testing focuses on verifying that the devices perform their designated tasks correctly and efficiently. This typically involves testing various aspects such as:

Protocol Compliance: Checking whether the networking device adheres to industry-standard protocols and specifications.

Configuration: Verifying that the device can be configured according to network requirements and that configuration changes are applied correctly.

Connectivity: Ensuring that the device can establish and maintain connections with other network devices, such as routers, switches, and endpoints.

Routing and Switching: Validating the routing and switching functionality of the device, including packet forwarding, VLAN configuration, and routing table updates.

Security Features: Testing security features such as access control lists (ACLs), firewalls, and intrusion prevention systems (IPS) to detect and prevent unauthorized access and malicious activities.

Non-functional Testing:

Non-functional testing focuses on aspects of networking devices that are not directly related to specific functions or features but are essential for overall system performance, reliability, and scalability. In the context of networking devices testing, non-functional testing encompasses various quality attributes, including:

Performance Testing: Assessing the performance characteristics of the networking device under different load conditions, such as bandwidth utilization, latency, and throughput.

Reliability Testing: Evaluating the reliability and availability of the device by testing its resilience to failures, including hardware failures, software bugs, and environmental factors.

Scalability Testing: Testing the device's ability to handle increasing workloads and scale to accommodate growing network demands without compromising performance or stability.

Usability Testing: Assessing the usability and user experience of the device's management interface, including configuration, monitoring, and troubleshooting capabilities.

Security Testing: Verifying the effectiveness of the device's security measures in protecting against various threats and vulnerabilities, including denial-of-service (DoS) attacks, malware, and unauthorized access.

In summary, while functional testing focuses on validating specific functions and features of networking devices, non-functional testing addresses broader quality attributes related to performance, reliability, scalability, usability, and security. Both types of testing are essential for ensuring the overall effectiveness, efficiency, and robustness of network infrastructures.

CHAPTER 03
TYPES OF NETWORK TESTING

3.1. What is Functional Testing

Functional testing is a critical aspect of ensuring the reliability, performance, and security of network devices within a network infrastructure. In this comprehensive guide, we will explore functional testing in detail, using network devices as examples. We'll delve into the intricacies of functional testing, provide a step-by-step approach to conducting tests, and illustrate concepts with a triangle testbed topology. Let's begin by understanding the fundamentals of functional testing and its significance in network infrastructure.

3.1.1. Introduction to Functional Testing:

Functional testing involves evaluating the functionality of network devices to ensure they perform as expected according to predefined specifications and requirements. Network devices encompass a wide range of hardware components and software functionalities, including routers, switches, firewalls, access points, and more. Functional testing aims to validate these devices' capabilities in managing network traffic, enforcing security policies, and facilitating communication between devices. This test will perform mostly at the development phase.

3.1.2. Importance of Functional Testing:

Functional testing is essential for several reasons:

Reliability: Ensures that network devices operate reliably under normal operating conditions.

Performance: Verifies that devices can handle network traffic efficiently and without degradation.

Security: Validates security features and policies implemented on devices to protect against unauthorized access and attacks.

Compliance: Ensures adherence to industry standards and regulatory requirements governing network operations.

By conducting thorough functional testing, organizations can identify and rectify potential issues before they impact network performance, security, and reliability, thus minimizing downtime and enhancing user experience.

3.1.3. Single, Triangle or four devices Testbed Topology:

To illustrate functional testing concepts, we'll use a various testbed topology consisting of one/three or four network devices interconnected in a Single/triangular or rectangular arrangement. Each device represents a different type of network device, such as a router, switch, or firewall. These topologies allow us to simulate various network scenarios and test the functionality of each device under different conditions.

3.1.4. Packet Flow Explanation:

In the triangle testbed topology, data packets flow between devices connected to different network devices. For example, if a device connected to the router sends data to a device connected to the switch, the router examines the destination IP address and forwards the packet to the appropriate interface based on routing table entries. The switch then receives the packet and forwards it to the destination device based on its MAC address. Understanding packet flow is essential for designing effective functional tests and diagnosing network issues.

3.1.5. Insides of Functional Testing:

Functional testing of network devices involves several key aspects:

a. Configuration Testing:
- Verify that devices are configured correctly according to network requirements.
- Test configuration settings for routing, switching, VLANs, access control, and other functionalities.

b. Traffic Handling Testing:
- Test the device's ability to handle different types of network traffic, including data, voice, and video.
- Evaluate packet forwarding performance, throughput, and latency under various traffic loads.

c. Security Feature Testing:
- Validate security features such as access control lists (ACLs), firewalls, intrusion prevention systems (IPS), and encryption.
- Test security policies to ensure they are correctly enforced and protect against common threats.

d. Protocol Conformance Testing:
- Verify that devices adhere to industry-standard protocols such as TCP/IP, OSPF, BGP, and SNMP.
- Test protocol interoperability with other devices and compatibility with third-party solutions.

e. High Availability Testing:
- Test device redundancy and failover mechanisms to ensure continuous operation in case of hardware or software failures.
- Evaluate convergence times and recovery procedures for different failure scenarios.

3.1.6. Conclusion:

Functional testing plays a crucial role in maintaining the integrity and performance of network devices within a network infrastructure. By conducting comprehensive functional testing, organizations can identify potential issues, optimize device configurations, and ensure a reliable and secure network environment. These single/triangular or rectangular testbed topologies provide a practical environment for simulating real-world network scenarios and testing device functionality under different conditions. By following best practices and leveraging appropriate testing tools, network administrators can enhance the reliability, performance, and security of their network devices, thus ensuring seamless communication and connectivity for users.

3.2. What is Performance Testing

Performance testing is a critical aspect of evaluating the capabilities and limitations of network devices within a network infrastructure. In this comprehensive guide, we will delve into the intricacies of performance testing, focusing on network devices such as routers, switches, firewalls, and access points. We'll explore the key aspects of performance testing, provide detailed insights into performance metrics and methodologies, and illustrate concepts with practical examples. Let's begin by understanding the fundamentals of performance testing and its significance in network infrastructure.

3.2.1. Introduction to Performance Testing:

Performance testing involves assessing the speed, throughput, latency, scalability, and reliability of network devices under various conditions and workloads. It aims to measure the device's ability to handle network traffic efficiently, maintain optimal performance levels, and meet user expectations. Performance testing is essential for identifying bottlenecks, optimizing configurations, and ensuring the overall health and stability of the network infrastructure.

3.2.2. Importance of Performance Testing:

Performance testing is crucial for several reasons:

Optimization: Identifies performance bottlenecks and optimization opportunities to improve network efficiency and responsiveness.

Capacity Planning: Helps predict and plan for future capacity requirements based on current and projected traffic loads.

User Experience: Ensures a satisfactory user experience by minimizing latency, packet loss, and downtime.

Resilience: Validates device resilience and failover mechanisms to maintain performance under adverse conditions.

By conducting thorough performance testing, organizations can proactively address performance issues, optimize network resources, and enhance the overall reliability and scalability of their network infrastructure.

3.2.3. Performance Metrics and Methodologies:

Performance testing involves measuring various metrics to assess the device's performance characteristics:

a. Throughput:
- Measures the rate at which data is transmitted between devices, typically expressed in bits per second (bps) or packets per second (pps).

b. Latency:
- Measures the delay in the transmission of data packets between devices, typically expressed in milliseconds (ms).

c. Packet Loss:
- Measures the percentage of data packets lost during transmission, which can impact the reliability and quality of network communication.

d. Scalability:
- Measures the device's ability to handle increasing numbers of users, devices, or traffic loads without degradation in performance.

e. Jitter:
- Measures the variation in latency over time, which can affect the consistency and quality of real-time applications such as VoIP or video streaming.

Performance testing methodologies include:

Load Testing: Evaluates device performance under normal and peak traffic loads to determine throughput, latency, and response times.

Stress Testing: Pushes devices to their limits by increasing traffic loads beyond capacity to identify performance bottlenecks and failure points.

Soak Testing: Measures device performance over an extended period under sustained traffic loads to assess long-term stability and reliability.

Benchmarking: Compares device performance against industry standards or similar devices to identify areas for improvement and optimization.

3.2.4. Insides of Performance Testing:

Performance testing of network devices involves several key aspects:

a. Traffic Generation:

> ➢ Generate synthetic traffic using tools such as Iperf, Spirent, or ixia to simulate different types of network traffic and workloads.

b. Traffic Analysis:

> ➢ Capture and analyze network traffic using packet capture tools like Wireshark or tcpdump to measure performance metrics such as throughput, latency, and packet loss.

c. Resource Utilization:

> ➢ Monitor device resource utilization, including CPU, memory, and interface bandwidth, during performance tests to identify resource constraints and optimization opportunities.

d. Real-World Scenarios:

> ➢ Test device performance under real-world scenarios, such as peak hours, high-demand applications, or distributed user populations, to assess real-world performance.

e. Failure Recovery:

> ➢ Test device failover mechanisms and recovery procedures to ensure seamless operation and minimal downtime in case of hardware or software failures.

3.2.5. Conclusion:

Performance testing is essential for assessing and optimizing the performance of network devices within a network infrastructure. By conducting comprehensive performance testing, organizations can identify performance bottlenecks, optimize device configurations, and ensure the reliability and scalability of their network infrastructure. Leveraging performance testing methodologies and tools enables organizations to proactively address performance issues, enhance user experience, and maintain a competitive edge in today's digital landscape.

3.3. What is Security Testing

Security testing is a critical aspect of evaluating the resilience and effectiveness of network devices within a network infrastructure. In this comprehensive guide, we will delve into the intricacies of security testing, focusing on network devices such as routers, switches, firewalls, and access points. We'll explore the key aspects of security testing, provide detailed insights into security vulnerabilities and testing methodologies, and illustrate concepts with practical examples. Let's begin by understanding the fundamentals of security testing and its significance in network infrastructure.

3.3.1. Introduction to Security Testing:

Security testing involves assessing the security posture of network devices to identify vulnerabilities, weaknesses, and misconfigurations that could be exploited by attackers. It aims to validate the effectiveness of security controls, policies, and mechanisms implemented on network devices to protect against unauthorized access, data breaches, and cyberattacks. Security testing encompasses a wide range of techniques, including vulnerability assessment, penetration testing, and security policy validation.

3.3.2. Importance of Security Testing:

Security testing is crucial for several reasons:

Risk Mitigation: Identifies security vulnerabilities and weaknesses that could be exploited by attackers to compromise network integrity and confidentiality.

Compliance: Ensures adherence to regulatory requirements and industry standards governing data security and privacy.

Trustworthiness: Validates the trustworthiness and reliability of network devices in protecting sensitive information and critical assets.

Resilience: Enhances the resilience and robustness of network infrastructure against evolving cyber threats and attack vectors.

By conducting thorough security testing, organizations can proactively detect and remediate security vulnerabilities, strengthen their security posture, and mitigate the risk of security breaches and data loss.

3.3.3. Security Testing Methodologies:

Security testing encompasses various methodologies and techniques to assess the security of network devices:

a. Vulnerability Assessment:

- Identifies known security vulnerabilities and weaknesses in network devices by scanning for software flaws, misconfigurations, and outdated firmware.
- Utilizes automated scanning tools such as Nessus, OpenVAS, or Qualys to identify vulnerabilities and prioritize remediation efforts.

b. Penetration Testing:

- Simulates real-world cyberattacks to assess the effectiveness of security controls and mechanisms in preventing unauthorized access and data breaches.
- Involves ethical hacking techniques to exploit identified vulnerabilities and gain unauthorized access to network devices.

c. Security Policy Validation:
- Validates the implementation and enforcement of security policies, access controls, and authentication mechanisms on network devices.
- Verifies compliance with security standards such as CIS benchmarks, NIST guidelines, or industry-specific regulations.

d. Threat Modeling:
- Identifies potential security threats, attack vectors, and risk scenarios specific to network devices and their configurations.
- Helps prioritize security testing efforts and allocate resources effectively to mitigate the most critical security risks.

3.3.4. Insides of Security Testing:

Security testing of network devices involves several key aspects:

a. Configuration Review:
- Review device configurations to identify insecure settings, default passwords, unnecessary services, and other configuration weaknesses.
- Ensure adherence to security best practices and hardening guidelines provided by device manufacturers and security standards bodies.

b. Access Control Testing:
- Test access controls, authentication mechanisms, and authorization policies implemented on network devices to prevent unauthorized access.
- Verify that only authorized users and devices have access to sensitive resources and functionalities.

c. Encryption and Cryptography:
- Assess the implementation of encryption and cryptographic protocols (e.g., SSL/TLS, IPsec) on network devices to protect data in transit and ensure confidentiality and integrity.
- Verify proper key management practices and certificate handling to prevent cryptographic vulnerabilities.

d. Firewall and Intrusion Detection/Prevention:
- Test firewall rules, intrusion detection/prevention systems (IDS/IPS), and other network security appliances to detect and prevent malicious activities.
- Validate the effectiveness of firewall policies and rule sets in filtering inbound and outbound traffic and detecting suspicious behavior.

3.3.5. Conclusion:

Security testing is essential for assessing and improving the security posture of network devices within a network infrastructure. By conducting comprehensive security testing, organizations can identify and remediate security vulnerabilities, strengthen access controls, and enhance the overall resilience and trustworthiness of their network infrastructure. Leveraging security testing methodologies and tools enables organizations to proactively defend against cyber threats, protect sensitive information, and maintain the integrity and confidentiality of their network assets.

3.4. What is Compatibility Testing

Compatibility testing involves verifying that network devices can coexist and operate effectively with other components, including hardware, software, protocols, and configurations. It aims to ensure seamless interoperability, data exchange, and functionality between network devices and their ecosystem, thereby minimizing integration challenges, configuration conflicts, and performance issues. Compatibility testing encompasses a wide range of scenarios, including device compatibility with network protocols, operating systems, security mechanisms, and management platforms.

Compatibility testing is crucial in ensuring seamless interoperability and integration of network devices within a network infrastructure. In this comprehensive guide, we will delve into the intricacies of compatibility testing, focusing on network devices such as routers, firewalls, load balancers, and their compatibility with other components such as Active Directory, network protocols, and third-party applications. We'll explore the key aspects of compatibility testing, provide detailed insights into compatibility issues and testing methodologies, and illustrate concepts with practical examples. Let's begin by understanding the fundamentals of compatibility testing and its significance in network infrastructure.

3.4.1. Importance of Compatibility Testing:

Compatibility testing is crucial for several reasons:

Interoperability: Validates that network devices can communicate and exchange data with other components within the network ecosystem.

Integration: Ensures seamless integration of network devices with existing infrastructure, applications, and services.

Configuration Management: Minimizes configuration conflicts and compatibility issues that could disrupt network operations or compromise security.

User Experience: Enhances user experience by enabling smooth interaction and functionality across diverse network environments.

By conducting thorough compatibility testing, organizations can mitigate the risk of compatibility issues, ensure the reliability and performance of network devices, and enhance the overall interoperability and functionality of their network infrastructure.

3.4.2. Compatibility Testing Scenarios:

Compatibility testing encompasses various scenarios and dimensions of compatibility, including:

a. Protocol Compatibility:

- Verifies that network devices support industry-standard protocols such as TCP/IP, DHCP, DNS, SNMP, and OSPF, ensuring interoperability with other network components.
- Tests compatibility with proprietary protocols and extensions used by specific vendors or applications.

b. Hardware Compatibility:

- Ensures compatibility with hardware components such as network interface cards (NICs), cables, connectors, and peripherals.
- Validates compatibility with different hardware platforms, architectures, and form factors.

c. Software Compatibility:

- Validates compatibility with operating systems, device drivers, firmware versions, and software applications running on network devices.
- Tests compatibility with third-party software solutions, management tools, and utilities used for network administration and monitoring.

d. Configuration Compatibility:

- Verifies compatibility with configuration settings, parameters, and policies applied to network devices, such as VLAN configurations, routing tables, and access control lists (ACLs).
- Tests compatibility with configuration management tools and automation frameworks used for deploying and managing network configurations.

3.4.3. Insides of Compatibility Testing:

Compatibility testing of network devices involves several key aspects:

a. Integration Testing:

- Test the integration of network devices with other components within the network ecosystem, such as routers, switches, firewalls, and load balancers.
- Verify seamless communication and functionality between interconnected devices, ensuring data exchange and traffic routing.

b. Protocol Interoperability Testing:

- Test compatibility with network protocols and standards to ensure interoperability with devices from different vendors and adherence to industry standards.

➤ Validate protocol implementations, packet formats, and error handling mechanisms across diverse network environments.

c. System Compatibility Testing:

➤ Validate compatibility with operating systems, device drivers, and software applications running on network devices, ensuring smooth operation and functionality.

➤ Test compatibility with different versions of operating systems, patches, and updates to minimize compatibility issues and software conflicts.

d. Security Compatibility Testing:

➤ Verify compatibility with security mechanisms such as firewalls, intrusion detection/prevention systems (IDS/IPS), and encryption protocols.

➤ Ensure that security policies, access controls, and encryption algorithms are compatible with network devices and do not compromise security posture.

3.4.4. Conclusion:

Compatibility testing is essential for ensuring the seamless interoperability and integration of network devices within a network infrastructure. By conducting comprehensive compatibility testing, organizations can minimize compatibility issues, ensure the reliability and performance of network devices, and enhance the overall interoperability and functionality of their network infrastructure. Leveraging compatibility testing methodologies and tools enables organizations to proactively address compatibility challenges, streamline integration processes, and optimize the efficiency and effectiveness of their network ecosystem.

3.5. What is Stress Testing

Stress testing is a critical aspect of evaluating the performance, reliability, and resilience of network devices within a network infrastructure. In this comprehensive guide, we will delve into the intricacies of stress testing, focusing on network devices such as routers, switches, firewalls, and load balancers. We'll explore the key aspects of stress testing, provide detailed insights into stress testing methodologies, scenarios, and tools, and illustrate concepts with practical examples. Let's begin by understanding the fundamentals of stress testing and its significance in network infrastructure.

3.5.1. Introduction to Stress Testing:

Stress testing involves subjecting network devices to extreme conditions and workloads to assess their performance, stability, and robustness under stress. It aims to identify the breaking points, limitations, and failure modes of network devices when subjected to high traffic loads, resource exhaustion, or adverse conditions. Stress testing helps validate device resilience, scalability, and failover mechanisms, enabling organizations to optimize their network infrastructure and mitigate the risk of performance degradation or downtime during peak usage periods or cyberattacks.

3.5.2. Importance of Stress Testing:

Stress testing is crucial for several reasons:

Performance Optimization: Identifies performance bottlenecks, scalability limitations, and resource constraints that could impact network performance under stress.

Failure Prevention: Proactively detects potential points of failure, instability, or degradation in network devices, enabling organizations to implement preemptive measures and safeguards.

Capacity Planning: Helps organizations anticipate and plan for future capacity requirements based on stress test results and performance data.

Resilience Enhancement: Validates device resilience, failover mechanisms, and recovery procedures to ensure continuous operation and minimal disruption during stress conditions.

By conducting thorough stress testing, organizations can optimize network performance, enhance device resilience, and ensure the reliability and availability of their network infrastructure under adverse conditions.

3.5.3. Stress Testing Methodologies:

Stress testing encompasses various methodologies and techniques to assess the performance and resilience of network devices:

a. Traffic Generation:

- Simulates high traffic loads using traffic generation tools such as Iperf, Spirent, or ixia to stress test network devices' throughput, latency, and packet processing capabilities.
- Generates different types of traffic patterns, including TCP, UDP, HTTP, and ICMP, to emulate real-world usage scenarios and stress network resources.

b. Resource Exhaustion:

- Stress tests device resources such as CPU, memory, and interface bandwidth to assess resource utilization, saturation points, and performance degradation under stress.
- Generates synthetic workloads, such as packet flooding or continuous data transfers, to exhaust device resources and identify resource bottlenecks.

c. Failure Simulation:

- Simulates failure scenarios, such as link failures, hardware malfunctions, or denial-of-service (DoS) attacks, to assess device resilience, failover mechanisms, and recovery procedures.
- Validates device response to failure events, including failover time, data loss, and impact on network operations.

d. Longevity Testing:

- ➤ Conducts stress tests over an extended period to assess device stability, reliability, and performance consistency under sustained stress conditions.
- ➤ Validates device endurance and longevity, ensuring continuous operation and minimal degradation over time.

3.5.4. Insides of Stress Testing:

Stress testing of network devices involves several key aspects:

a. Performance Metrics Analysis:

- ➤ Analyzes performance metrics such as throughput, latency, packet loss, and resource utilization during stress tests to identify performance bottlenecks and limitations.
- ➤ Establishes baseline performance metrics and thresholds for comparison and evaluation.

b. Failure Mode Analysis:

- ➤ Identifies failure modes, error conditions, and performance degradation patterns observed during stress tests to understand device behavior under stress.
- ➤ Classifies failure modes based on severity, impact, and frequency to prioritize remediation efforts and risk mitigation strategies.

c. Scalability Assessment:

- ➤ Measures device scalability and capacity to handle increasing traffic loads, device counts, or concurrent connections without degradation in performance or stability.
- ➤ Evaluates scalability limits and constraints to inform capacity planning and infrastructure scaling decisions.

d. Recovery Validation:

- ➤ Validates device recovery mechanisms, failover procedures, and recovery time objectives (RTOs) to ensure rapid and seamless recovery from stress-induced failures or disruptions.
- ➤ Tests device resilience to various failure scenarios, including hardware failures, software crashes, and network anomalies.

3.5.5. Conclusion:

Stress testing is essential for evaluating the performance, resilience, and reliability of network devices within a network infrastructure. By conducting comprehensive stress testing, organizations can identify performance bottlenecks, validate device resilience, and optimize their network infrastructure to withstand high traffic loads, resource exhaustion, and adverse conditions. Leveraging stress testing methodologies and tools enables organizations to proactively address performance issues, enhance device resilience, and ensure the reliability and availability of their network infrastructure under stress.

CHAPTER 04
TEST PLANNING AND STRATEGY

4.1. Defining Objectives and Scope

Test planning is a crucial phase in the overall testing process, where objectives and scope are defined to ensure that testing efforts align with organizational goals and requirements. In this section, we'll explore the importance of defining objectives and scope in test planning, along with best practices and considerations.

4.1.1. Importance of Defining Objectives and Scope:

a. Alignment with Goals:
- Defining clear objectives ensures that testing efforts are aligned with the organization's goals and objectives. It helps prioritize testing activities based on business priorities and critical functionalities.

b. Focus and Direction:
- Clearly defined objectives provide focus and direction to testing efforts, guiding testers on what needs to be tested and why. It helps avoid scope creep and ensures that testing stays on track.

c. Risk Management:
- Objectives and scope definition allows for identification and mitigation of risks associated with testing. It helps prioritize testing activities based on risk exposure and criticality.

d. Resource Optimization:
- By clearly defining objectives and scope, resources can be allocated efficiently to areas that are most critical to the project's success. It helps optimize resource utilization and maximize testing effectiveness.

4.1.2. Best Practices for Defining Objectives and Scope:

a. Collaboration:
- Involve stakeholders from various departments, including business, development, and testing, in defining objectives and scope. Collaborative discussions ensure that all perspectives are considered.

b. Clarity and Specificity:
- Objectives should be clear, specific, and measurable. Avoid vague language or ambiguous goals. Use SMART criteria (Specific, Measurable, Achievable, Relevant, Time-bound) to define objectives.

c. Prioritization:

> ➤ Prioritize objectives based on business value, criticality, and risk. Identify high-priority functionalities or features that must be tested first to ensure project success.

d. Scope Boundaries:

> ➤ Clearly define the boundaries of the testing scope to avoid ambiguity and scope creep. Document what is included and excluded from the testing scope to manage expectations effectively.

4.1.3. Considerations for Defining Objectives and Scope:

a. Project Constraints:

> ➤ Consider project constraints such as time, budget, and resources when defining objectives and scope. Ensure that objectives are realistic and achievable within project constraints.

b. Regulatory Requirements:

> ➤ Take into account regulatory requirements, industry standards, and compliance mandates when defining objectives and scope. Ensure that testing activities address relevant regulatory concerns.

c. Stakeholder Expectations:

> ➤ Understand and manage stakeholder expectations regarding testing objectives and scope. Communicate clearly with stakeholders to ensure alignment and buy-in.

d. Flexibility:

> ➤ Maintain flexibility in objectives and scope to accommodate changes or unforeseen circumstances. Be prepared to adapt and adjust testing priorities based on evolving project needs.

4.1.4. Conclusion:

Defining objectives and scope is a critical aspect of test planning, providing focus, direction, and clarity to testing efforts. By aligning testing objectives with organizational goals, prioritizing critical functionalities, and clearly defining scope boundaries, testing teams can optimize resource utilization, mitigate risks, and ensure project success. Effective collaboration, clarity, prioritization, and consideration of project constraints and stakeholder expectations are essential for defining objectives and scope that drive successful testing outcomes.

4.2. Identifying Key Components

In test planning and strategy, identifying key components is essential to ensure comprehensive coverage and effective execution of testing activities. These components serve as the building blocks for defining test objectives, scope, and strategies. Let's explore some of the key components along with examples:

4.2.1. Test Objectives:

Test objectives define the goals and purpose of testing activities. They provide direction and focus to testing efforts, ensuring alignment with project goals and requirements. Examples of test objectives include:

Verify Functionality: Ensure that all critical features and functionalities of the system work as expected.

Assess Performance: Evaluate system performance under various load conditions to identify bottlenecks and optimize performance.

Validate Security: Confirm that the system is secure against unauthorized access, data breaches, and cyber threats.

Ensure Compatibility: Verify compatibility with different devices, platforms, browsers, and operating systems to ensure seamless integration.

Assure Reliability: Validate system reliability and stability under normal and stress conditions to minimize downtime and disruptions.

4.2.2. Test Scope:

Test scope defines the boundaries and extent of testing activities. It outlines what will be tested, including features, functionalities, and environments. Examples of test scope components include:

Functional Coverage: Specify which features and functionalities will be tested, including both core and edge cases.

Platform Coverage: Identify the platforms, operating systems, browsers, and devices that will be included in testing.

Integration Points: Determine the interfaces, APIs, and third-party integrations that will be tested for compatibility and functionality.

Data Coverage: Define the types of data, scenarios, and datasets that will be used in testing, including both valid and invalid data.

4.2.3. Test Strategy:

Test strategy outlines the approach and methodologies that will be used to achieve testing objectives within the defined scope. It provides guidelines for planning, designing, executing, and reporting on testing activities. Examples of test strategy components include:

Testing Techniques: Specify the testing techniques, such as manual testing, automated testing, exploratory testing, and regression testing, that will be employed.

Test Levels: Define the testing levels, including unit testing, integration testing, system testing, and acceptance testing, that will be performed.

Risk-based Testing: Identify and prioritize risks based on their impact and likelihood, focusing testing efforts on high-risk areas.

Test Environment: Describe the test environment setup, including hardware, software, tools, and configurations required for testing.

4.2.4. Test Deliverables:

Test deliverables are the artifacts and documentation produced during the testing process. They provide stakeholders with insights into testing progress, results, and findings. Examples of test deliverables include:

Test Plan: Document outlining the objectives, scope, approach, and schedule of testing activities.

Test Cases: Detailed instructions for executing test scenarios, including inputs, expected outputs, and test conditions.

Test Reports: Summaries of testing results, including defects, issues, and metrics such as test coverage and pass/fail status.

Traceability Matrix: Matrix linking test cases to requirements, ensuring comprehensive coverage and validation.

4.2.5. Conclusion:

Identifying key components in test planning and strategy is essential for ensuring effective and efficient testing activities. By clearly defining test objectives, scope, strategy, and deliverables, testing teams can align their efforts with project goals, mitigate risks, and deliver high-quality software products that meet user expectations. Effective communication, collaboration, and documentation are essential for successful identification and implementation of key testing components.

4.3. Developing Test Cases

Developing test cases is a critical aspect of test planning and strategy for network testing. Test cases serve as detailed instructions for executing testing activities and verifying the functionality, performance, and security of network devices. In this section, we'll develop test cases for network testing, including examples that cover various aspects of device functionality.

4.3.1. Connectivity Testing:

Test Case 1: Ping Test

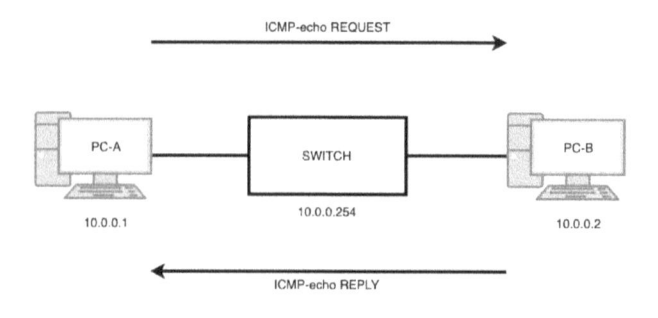

Fig-4.3.1.1: Ping Test

Objective: Verify basic connectivity between devices.

Steps:

Send ICMP ping packets from PC A to PC B through Switch-1.

Verify that PC B responds to ping requests from PC A.

Expected Result: Ping responses should be received within an acceptable timeframe (e.g., <10 ms).

Test Case 2: Link Status

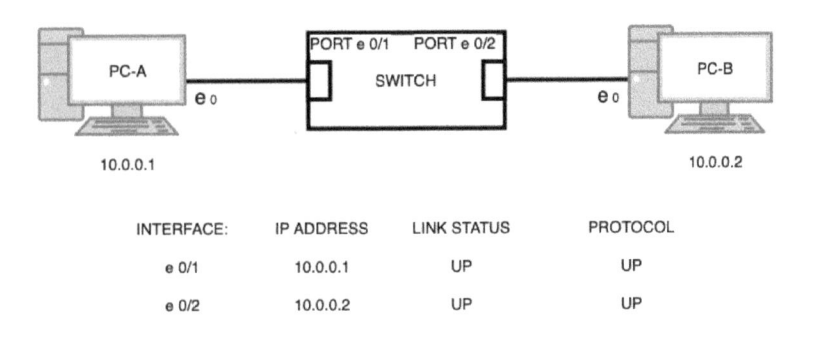

Fig-4.3.1.2: Link Status

Objective: Validate link status and interface connectivity.

Steps:

Check the status of network interfaces on Switch for PC-A and PC-B.

Verify that all interfaces are up and operational.

Expected Result: All network interfaces should be in an up state with no errors or issues.

4.3.2. Configuration Testing:

Test Case 3: VLAN Configuration

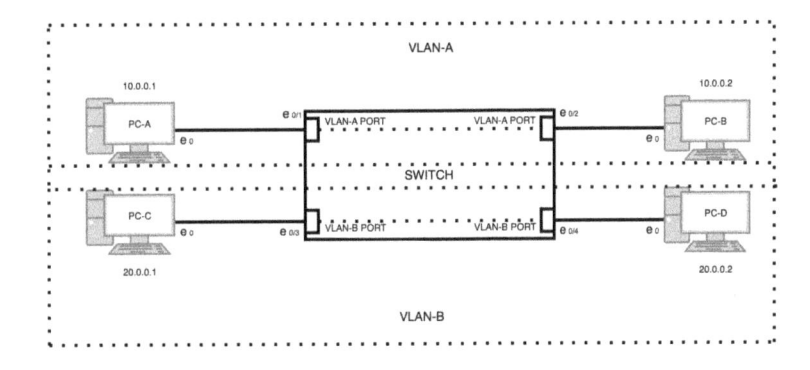

Fig-4.3.2.1: VLAN Configuration

Objective: Validate VLAN configuration and segmentation.

Steps:

Create VLAN-A & B on Switch-1.

Assign Switch-1 Port e0/1 to PC-A and configure in VLAN-A

Assign Switch-1 Port e0/2 to PC-B and configure in VLAN-A

Assign Switch-1 Port e0/3 to PC-C and configure in VLAN-B

Assign Switch-1 Port e0/4 to PC-D and configure in VLAN-B

Verify link status of assign specific ports to VLANs and verify segregation.

Expected Result: PC's in different VLANs should not be able to communicate with each other and PC's in the same VLAN should be able to communicate(ping) each other.

Test Case 4: Routing Configuration

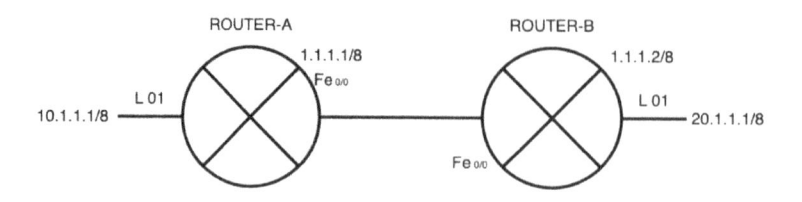

Fig-4.3.2.2: VLAN Configuration

Objective: Verify routing functionality and routing table entries.

Steps:

Configure loopback interface lo1 on Router A. Configure loopback on RouterB.

Configure dynamic routing protocol OSPF on Router A and RouterB

Advertise Loopback interface on each router into OSPF routing protocol

Verify that Router A loopback network can be seen in Router B routing table and vise-versa

Expected Result: Router A should see Router B loopback network in OSPF routing table and be able to ping it and Router B should see Router A loopback network in OSPF routing table and should be able to ping it.

4.3.3. Performance Testing:

Test Case 5: Bandwidth Testing

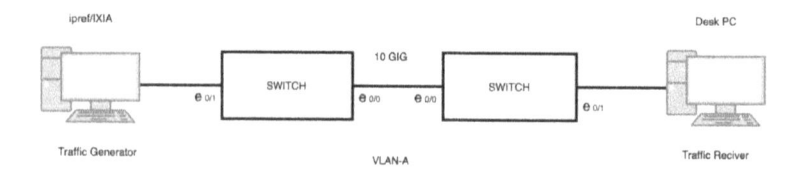

Fig-4.3.3.1: VLAN Configuration

Objective: Measure bandwidth capacity and throughput.

Steps:

Connect Traffic generator to Switch A and connect receiver PC to Switch B port

Generate Traffic (Iperf/IXIA) and measure the throughput between the ports connected to both switches.

Measure the throughput and bandwidth utilization and compare with the line speed of the links..

Expected Result: The measured throughput should match to the link/port speed bandwidth capacity.

Test Case 6: Latency Measurement

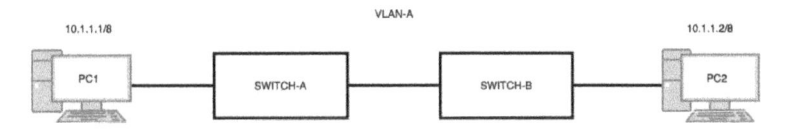

Fig-4.3.3.2: Latency Measurement

Objective: Evaluate latency and packet delay.

Steps:

Send packets between PC 1 and PC 2.

Measure the round-trip time (RTT) for packet transmission.

Expected Result: Latency should be within acceptable limits (e.g., <50 ms).

4.3.4. Security Testing:

Test Case 7: MAC Access Control

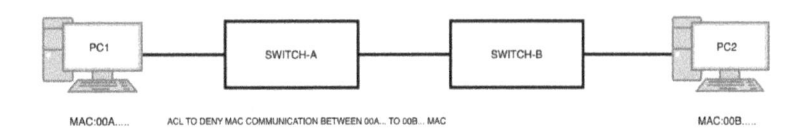

Fig-4.3.4.1: MAC Access Control

Objective: Verify MAC access control mechanisms.

Steps:

Connect PC1 to Switch A and PC2 to Switch B

Configure MAC access control rule on Switch A to deny any communication between MAC: 00A.. To MAC:00B..

Attempt to access PC2 from PC1

Verify that access is denied.

Expected Result: Unauthorized users should be prevented from accessing restricted resources.

Test Case 8: Firewall Rules

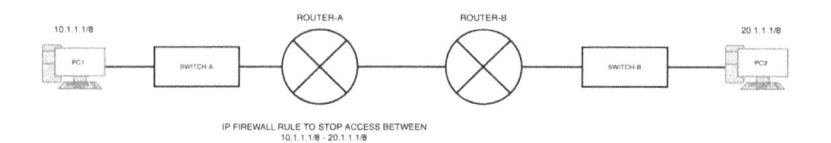

Fig-4.3.4.2: Firewall Rules

Objective: Validate firewall rule enforcement.

Steps:

Connect PC1 to Switch A to Router B on LAN and connect PC2 to Switch B to Router B on LAN

Connect both routers on WAN connection.

Configure firewall rules on Router A to block 10.0.0.0/8 network to 20.0.0.0/8 network traffic.

Attempt to send blocked traffic to PC1 to PC2.

Expected Result: Blocked traffic should be dropped or denied by the firewall rule.

4.3.5. Device Functionality Testing:

Test Case 9: Switch Port speed and Vlan Configuration

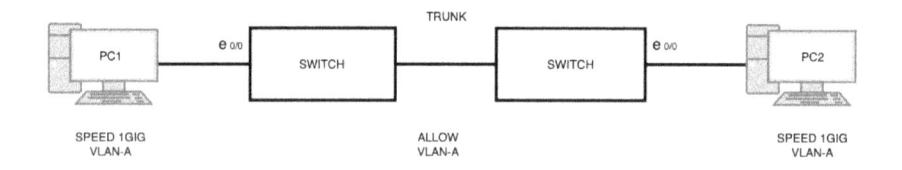

Fig-4.3.5.1: Switch Port speed and Vlan Configuration

Objective: Verify switch port functionality and configuration.

Steps:

Configure VLAN membership, port modes, speed and spanning tree protocol settings on a switch A port e0/0 and on Switch B port e0/0.

Connect a PC1 & PC2 to the configured port and verify connectivity.

Expected Result: The device should be able to communicate over the configured switch port.

Test Case 10: Firewall NAT Configuration

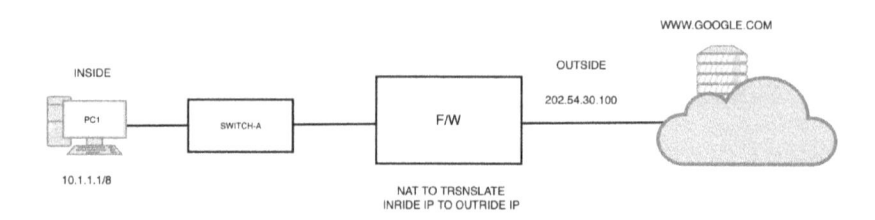

Fig-4.3.5.2: Firewall NAT Configuration

Objective: Validate Network Address Translation (NAT) functionality on a firewall.

Steps:

Connect PC1 to Switch A to Firewall A.

Configure inside IP on PC1 and configure Outside public IP con Firewall A

Configure NAT rules on the firewall to translate internal IP addresses to external IP addresses.

Verify that internal PC1 can access external www.goole.com site using NAT translations.

Expected Result: Internal devices should be able to access www.google.com site via NAT translations.

4.3.6. Conclusion:

Developing comprehensive test cases is essential for ensuring thorough coverage and effective validation of network devices' functionality, performance, and security. By defining clear objectives, steps, and expected results for each test case, testing teams can systematically verify network functionality, identify potential issues, and ensure the reliability and integrity of the network infrastructure. Effective test planning and strategy, combined with well-developed test cases, are essential for delivering high-quality and reliable network solutions.

4.4. Creating Test Scenarios

Creating test scenarios involves defining realistic situations or events that mimic real-world conditions to validate the functionality, performance, and security of network devices. These scenarios help ensure comprehensive testing coverage and enable testers to assess the behavior of the network under various conditions. Below are examples of test scenarios for network testing, including a diverse range of network devices like switches, routers, firewalls, SDN controllers, wireless access points, VoIP systems, etc., along with illustrative topology examples.

4.4.1. Basic Connectivity Testing:

Below is the master consolidated end to end site (Site-A, Site-B and HeadQuarters) diagram with which we can do all the below scenarios

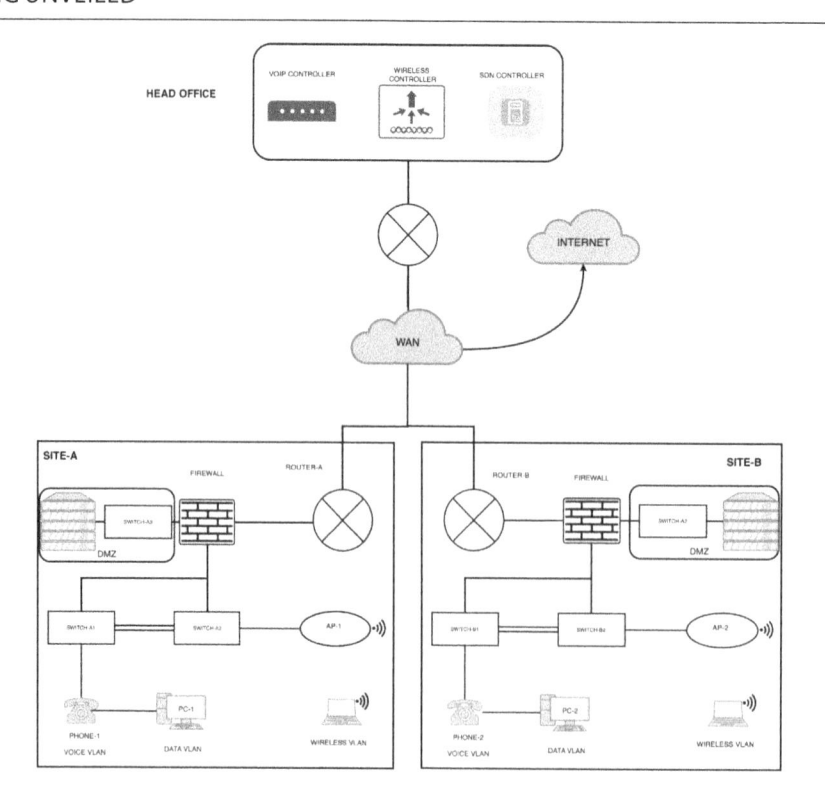

Fig-4.4.1.1: Full scenario including Site-A, Site-B & HeadQuarters

Scenario 1: Local Area Network (LAN) Connectivity

Topology: Simple LAN topology with multiple switches connected to a router/firewall.

Scenario: Verify basic connectivity between devices within the LAN.

Test Steps:

Connect multiple devices (e.g., PCs, servers) to different switch ports.

Ensure that devices can communicate with each other within the same LAN segment.

Expected Result: Devices should be able to ping each other and establish TCP/IP connections without issues.

4.4.2. VLAN Segmentation Testing:

Scenario 2: VLAN Segregation

Topology: VLAN-enabled network with multiple VLANs configured on switches.

Scenario: Validate VLAN segregation and inter-VLAN routing functionality.

Test Steps:

Configure VLANs on switches and assign ports to respective VLANs.

Verify that devices in different VLANs cannot communicate directly.

Test inter-VLAN routing by routing traffic through a router or Layer 3 switch.

Expected Result: Devices in different VLANs should be isolated, and inter-VLAN communication should be routed properly.

4.4.3. Security Policy Enforcement:

Scenario 3: Firewall Rules Validation

Topology: Network with a firewall deployed between LAN and WAN segments.

Scenario: Ensure that firewall rules are enforced correctly to filter inbound and outbound traffic.

Test Steps:

Define firewall rules to allow or deny specific traffic based on policies (e.g., allow HTTP traffic, deny ICMP).

Generate traffic that matches the defined rules (e.g., HTTP requests, ICMP ping).

Expected Result: Traffic should be allowed or denied according to the configured firewall rules.

4.4.4. Quality of Service (QoS) Testing:

Scenario 4: VoIP Traffic Prioritization

Topology: VoIP system connected to the LAN, with QoS policies implemented.

Scenario: Verify that VoIP traffic receives priority treatment over other types of traffic.

Test Steps:

Configure QoS policies to prioritize VoIP traffic (e.g., SIP, RTP) over data traffic.

Simulate high data traffic and VoIP calls concurrently.

Expected Result: VoIP calls should maintain acceptable voice quality, even under high network load, due to QoS prioritization.

4.4.5. Software-Defined Networking (SDN) Testing:

Scenario 5: SDN Controller Redundancy

Topology: SDN-enabled network with multiple SDN controllers deployed for redundancy.

Scenario: Validate failover and redundancy mechanisms of SDN controllers.

Test Steps:

Configure multiple SDN controllers in an active-standby or active-active mode.

Simulate a failure of the active SDN controller and observe failover behavior.

Expected Result: Traffic should seamlessly failover to the standby SDN controller without interruption.

4.4.6. Wireless Network Testing:

Scenario 6: Wireless Coverage and Roaming

Topology: Wireless LAN (WLAN) with multiple access points (APs) deployed.

Scenario: Assess wireless coverage, signal strength, and client roaming behavior.

Test Steps:

Walk through different areas of the WLAN coverage area and measure signal strength.

Test client roaming by moving devices between AP coverage areas.

Expected Result: Clients should maintain connectivity and seamlessly roam between APs without disconnection.

4.4.7. Conclusion:

Creating diverse test scenarios for network testing is essential for ensuring comprehensive coverage and validating the functionality, performance, and security of network devices. By simulating real-world conditions and events, testers can identify potential issues, assess network behavior, and ensure the reliability and integrity of the network infrastructure. Effective test planning and strategy, combined with well-defined test scenarios, are essential for delivering high-quality and resilient network solutions.

CHAPTER 05

TEST TOOLS AND TECHNOLOGIES

5.1. Overview of Network Testing Tools

Network testing tools play a crucial role in validating the functionality, performance, and security of network devices and infrastructure. They provide testers with the necessary capabilities to conduct comprehensive testing and troubleshooting across various network environments. Below is a list of industry-standard network testing tools along with proprietary tools used by product companies and those utilized by system integration firms:

5.1.1. Industry-Standard Testing Tools:

I. Wireshark:

Deployment: Wireshark is a widely-used network protocol analyzer deployed across various network environments, including enterprise networks, data centers, and telecommunications networks.

Description: Wireshark allows users to capture, analyze, and troubleshoot network traffic in real-time. It supports a wide range of protocols and provides detailed packet-level insights into network communication.

II. Iperf:

Deployment: Iperf is commonly deployed in network performance testing scenarios, including WAN optimization, bandwidth testing, and throughput measurement.

Description: Iperf is a command-line tool used to measure network bandwidth, throughput, and latency by generating TCP and UDP traffic between two endpoints. It is often used for assessing network performance and capacity planning.

III. Nmap:

Deployment: Nmap is utilized for network discovery, port scanning, and vulnerability assessment across diverse network environments, including corporate networks, data centers, and cloud environments.

Description: Nmap is a powerful network scanning tool that helps identify active hosts, open ports, and services running on network devices. It is commonly used for security testing and network reconnaissance.

IV. Nagios:

Deployment: Nagios is employed for network monitoring, alerting, and performance management in enterprise IT environments, including data centers, server rooms, and cloud infrastructure.

Description: Nagios provides comprehensive monitoring capabilities for network devices, servers, applications, and services. It helps detect and alert on network issues, performance degradation, and service outages.

V. IXIA:

Deployment: IXIA is used in a variety of network testing scenarios, including performance testing, security testing, and network validation, across enterprise networks, service providers, and equipment manufacturers.

Description: IXIA offers a range of network testing solutions that simulate real-world traffic and conditions. It provides detailed performance metrics, helps identify vulnerabilities, and validates the resilience and capacity of network devices and infrastructures. IXIA's comprehensive testing capabilities make it a preferred tool for both pre-deployment and ongoing network assessments.

5.1.2. Proprietary Tools:

I. Cisco Packet Tracer:

Deployment: Cisco Packet Tracer is a proprietary network simulation tool used by Cisco for network design, configuration, and troubleshooting in Cisco-centric environments, such as enterprise networks and educational institutions.

Description: Cisco Packet Tracer allows users to create virtual network topologies, configure Cisco devices, and simulate network behavior. It is commonly used for training, certification preparation, and prototyping.

II. Juniper Junos Space:

Deployment: Junos Space is a proprietary network management platform developed by Juniper Networks for managing Juniper devices and network infrastructure in enterprise and service provider environments.

Description: Junos Space provides centralized management, configuration, monitoring, and automation capabilities for Juniper devices. It is used for provisioning, troubleshooting, and optimizing Juniper networks.

5.1.3. Tools Used by System Integration Companies:

I. Spirent TestCenter:

Deployment: Spirent TestCenter is a high-performance testing solution deployed by system integration firms and network equipment manufacturers (NEMs) for validating network infrastructure, including switches, routers, and firewalls.

Description: Spirent TestCenter offers a comprehensive suite of test capabilities, including traffic generation, protocol emulation, and performance testing. It is used for validating network devices, evaluating scalability, and assessing quality of service (QoS).

II. **Keysight IxNetwork:**

Deployment: Keysight IxNetwork is utilized by system integration companies for testing and validating network infrastructure, including Layer 2/3 switches, routers, and network appliances.

Description: IxNetwork provides scalable and realistic traffic emulation, protocol testing, and performance measurement capabilities. It is used for functional testing, interoperability testing, and benchmarking of network devices.

5.1.4. Conclusion:

Network testing tools encompass a diverse range of solutions tailored for various testing scenarios and environments. From industry-standard tools like Wireshark and Nmap to proprietary solutions like Cisco Packet Tracer and Juniper Junos Space, organizations have a plethora of options to choose from based on their specific requirements and infrastructure. System integration companies often leverage specialized tools like Spirent TestCenter and Keysight IxNetwork for comprehensive testing of network devices and infrastructure in complex deployments. Effective selection and deployment of network testing tools are essential for ensuring the reliability, performance, and security of modern network environments.

5.2. Popular Testing Frameworks

Testing frameworks provide a structured approach to conducting testing activities, streamlining test creation, execution, and reporting processes. In the realm of network testing, various frameworks cater to different aspects of testing, including functional testing, performance testing, and security testing. Below is a list of industry-standard testing frameworks, along with proprietary frameworks used by product companies and those employed by system integration firms:

5.2.1. Industry-Standard Testing Frameworks:

I. **Robot Framework:**

Deployment: Robot Framework is widely used for software testing, but we can also use it for automation in network testing scenarios, including functional testing of network protocols, device configurations, and API testing.

Description: Robot Framework offers a keyword-driven testing approach, making it suitable for both technical and non-technical testers. It supports a wide range of test libraries and integrations, facilitating comprehensive network testing.

II. PyTest:

Deployment: PyTest is commonly used for test automation in Python-based network testing projects, including unit testing, integration testing, and API testing.

Description: PyTest provides a simple and flexible testing framework for writing and executing test cases in Python. It offers powerful features such as fixtures, parameterization, and plugins, making it suitable for testing diverse network environments.

III. JUnit:

Deployment: JUnit is employed for unit testing and integration testing of Java-based network applications, middleware, and services.

Description: JUnit is a popular testing framework for Java developers, offering a simple and intuitive API for writing and executing test cases. It is commonly used for validating network application logic, APIs, and services.

5.2.2. Proprietary Testing Frameworks:

I. Cisco PyATS (Python Automation Framework):

Deployment: Cisco PyATS is a proprietary testing framework developed by Cisco for network automation, validation, and testing of Cisco devices and network infrastructure.

Description: PyATS provides a powerful and extensible framework for automating testing and validation tasks across Cisco devices and platforms. It offers built-in support for device configuration, testing automation, and result analysis.

II. Juniper Junos Automation Toolkit:

Deployment: Juniper Junos Automation Toolkit is a proprietary testing framework offered by Juniper Networks for automating testing and validation of Juniper devices and network services.

Description: Junos Automation Toolkit enables users to automate testing tasks, including configuration validation, compliance checking, and performance testing, across Juniper devices and platforms.

5.2.3. Frameworks Used by System Integrators:

I. Spirent TestCenter Automation Framework:

Deployment: Spirent TestCenter Automation Framework is utilized by system integration companies for automating testing and validation of network infrastructure, including switches, routers, and network appliances.

Description: Spirent TestCenter Automation Framework offers a comprehensive solution for automating test scenarios, traffic generation, and performance measurement in complex network deployments. It provides APIs and scripting support for customization and integration with test automation workflows.

7. Keysight Test Automation Platform (TAP):

Deployment: Keysight Test Automation Platform (TAP) is employed by system integration firms for automating testing tasks across diverse network environments and equipment.

Description: Keysight TAP offers a modular and scalable automation framework for test orchestration, execution, and result analysis. It provides support for multi-vendor environments, protocol testing, and integration with third-party tools and systems.

5.2.4. Conclusion:

Testing frameworks play a crucial role in automating and streamlining testing activities in network testing projects. From industry-standard frameworks like Robot Framework and PyTest to proprietary solutions like Cisco PyATS and Juniper Junos Automation Toolkit, organizations have a variety of options to choose from based on their specific requirements and infrastructure. System integration companies often leverage specialized frameworks like Spirent TestCenter Automation Framework and Keysight Test Automation Platform (TAP) for automating testing tasks and validating network infrastructure in complex deployments. Effective selection and deployment of testing frameworks are essential for enhancing testing efficiency, reducing time-to-market, and ensuring the reliability and performance of network solutions.

5.3. Automation in Network Testing

Automation plays a pivotal role in network testing by streamlining repetitive tasks, improving testing efficiency, and ensuring consistency in test execution. Leveraging automation tools and frameworks enables organizations to scale their testing efforts, reduce manual effort, and accelerate time-to-market for network solutions. Here are some ways automation contributes to network testing along with examples:

5.3.1. Configuration Management:

Example: Using automation scripts to provision and configure network devices such as switches, routers, and firewalls according to predefined templates or policies. Tools like Ansible, Puppet, or Chef automate the deployment and configuration of network devices, ensuring consistency and reducing human error.

5.3.2. Test Case Execution:

Example: Automating the execution of test cases for functional testing, performance testing, and security testing of network devices and infrastructure. Test automation frameworks such as Robot Framework, PyTest, or Selenium enable the creation of automated test scripts that validate network functionality, performance, and security across different scenarios and environments.

5.3.3. Traffic Generation:

Example: Automating the generation of network traffic to simulate real-world conditions and test network performance, scalability, and resilience. Tools like Ixia's IxNetwork or Spirent TestCenter offer traffic generation capabilities that enable testers to emulate various network traffic patterns, protocols, and loads for performance testing and capacity planning.

5.3.4. Continuous Integration and Deployment (CI/CD):

Example: Integrating network testing into CI/CD pipelines to automate the validation of network changes, configurations, and deployments. CI/CD tools like Jenkins, GitLab CI/CD, or CircleCI automate the execution of network tests as part of the software development lifecycle, ensuring that changes to network infrastructure are thoroughly tested before deployment.

5.3.5. Monitoring and Alerting:

Example: Automating the monitoring of network performance, availability, and security metrics in real-time and triggering alerts or notifications for anomalous behavior or performance degradation. Monitoring tools like Nagios, Zabbix, or Prometheus automate the collection and analysis of network data, enabling proactive management and troubleshooting.

5.3.6. Compliance and Security Auditing:

Example: Automating compliance checks and security audits to ensure adherence to regulatory requirements, industry standards, and security best practices. Tools like Nessus, Qualys, or Tenable automate vulnerability scanning, configuration auditing, and patch management across network devices, identifying and remediating security vulnerabilities.

5.3.7. Benefits of Automation in Network Testing

Efficiency: Automation reduces manual effort and enables testers to focus on higher-value activities, accelerating testing cycles and improving productivity.

Consistency: Automated tests ensure consistent test execution and results, reducing variability and increasing reliability in testing outcomes.

Scalability: Automation allows organizations to scale their testing efforts to meet the growing complexity and demands of network infrastructure and applications.

Reusability: Automated test scripts can be reused across different projects, environments, and scenarios, maximizing ROI and reducing time-to-market.

Risk Mitigation: Automation helps identify issues and vulnerabilities early in the development lifecycle, reducing the risk of deployment failures, outages, or security breaches.

5.3.8. Conclusion:

Automation revolutionizes network testing by enabling organizations to achieve higher levels of efficiency, consistency, scalability, and risk mitigation. By automating configuration management, test case execution, traffic generation, CI/CD integration, monitoring, compliance auditing, and security testing, organizations can ensure the reliability, performance, and security of their network infrastructure while accelerating time-to-market and reducing operational overhead. Effective adoption of automation tools and practices is essential for staying competitive and resilient in today's dynamic network environments.

5.4. Virtualization and Emulation

Virtualization and emulation technologies play a crucial role in network testing by providing a simulated environment for testing without the need for physical hardware. These technologies enable testers to replicate complex network scenarios, validate configurations, and assess performance in a controlled and scalable environment. Here's how we can introduce virtualization and emulation in testing, the types of tests we can perform, and the benefits, with a focus on scalability testing:

5.4.1. Introduction to Virtualization and Emulation:

Virtualization involves creating virtual instances of hardware, software, or networks, enabling multiple virtual environments to run on a single physical host. Emulation, on the other hand, replicates the behavior of real devices or systems in a software-based environment, allowing testers to simulate network conditions and scenarios.

Each product company often provides its own emulation version of their hardware products, such as Cisco, Juniper, and Arista routers. These emulated versions enable the creation of network topologies that match specific testing requirements, particularly for scalability testing. Using emulated environments is advantageous because setting up large testbeds with physical hardware can be challenging and resource-intensive. Emulation setups allow companies to efficiently test and validate scalability scenarios without the need for extensive physical infrastructure. This approach not only saves time and resources but also provides flexibility in testing various configurations and conditions.

5.4.2. Types of Tests with Virtualization and Emulation:

Functional Testing: Validating the functionality of network devices, protocols, and services in a simulated environment.

Performance Testing: Assessing the performance and scalability of network infrastructure under varying loads and conditions.

Security Testing: Evaluating the security posture of network devices and applications in a controlled environment.

Interoperability Testing: Testing the compatibility and interoperability of network devices, protocols, and services in a virtualized network environment.

Scalability Testing: Assessing the ability of network infrastructure to scale and handle increased workload and traffic volumes.

5.4.3. Benefits of Virtualization and Emulation:

Cost Savings: Virtualization reduces the need for physical hardware, leading to cost savings in equipment procurement, maintenance, and space requirements.

Flexibility: Virtualized environments can be easily replicated, modified, and scaled up or down to accommodate testing requirements.

Isolation: Virtualized environments provide isolation from production networks, allowing testers to conduct testing without impacting live systems.

Resource Optimization: Virtualization optimizes resource utilization by dynamically allocating resources based on demand, improving efficiency and performance.

Scalability: Virtualization and emulation enable scalability testing, allowing testers to assess the performance and scalability of network infrastructure under varying loads and conditions.

5.4.4. Scalability Testing with Virtualization and Emulation:

Example Scenario:

Suppose a company is deploying a new web application and needs to assess the scalability of the underlying network infrastructure to handle increased user traffic during peak periods.

Approach:

Virtualized Environment Setup: Create a virtualized network environment using tools like VMware, VirtualBox, or GNS3, simulating the production network topology.

Traffic Generation: Generate simulated user traffic using traffic generation tools like Iperf, Apache JMeter, or Spirent TestCenter, gradually increasing the load on the network.

Load Balancing: Introduce load balancing mechanisms using software-based load balancers like HAProxy or Nginx to distribute traffic across multiple servers.

Performance Monitoring: Monitor the performance metrics of network devices, servers, and applications using monitoring tools like Nagios, Zabbix, or Prometheus.

Scalability Testing: Increase the user traffic load incrementally and observe how the network infrastructure responds, assessing factors such as throughput, latency, and resource utilization.

Analysis and Optimization: Analyze the test results to identify bottlenecks, performance issues, or scalability limitations. Optimize the network configuration, scaling up resources as needed to improve performance and scalability.

5.4.5. Benefits of Scalability Testing with Virtualization and Emulation:

Risk Mitigation: Scalability testing helps identify performance bottlenecks and scalability limitations early in the development lifecycle, reducing the risk of service degradation or outages during peak periods.

Optimized Resource Allocation: By assessing the scalability of network infrastructure, organizations can optimize resource allocation, ensuring that sufficient resources are available to handle increased workload and traffic volumes.

Improved User Experience: Scalability testing ensures that the network infrastructure can accommodate growing user demand without sacrificing performance or user experience, enhancing customer satisfaction and retention.

Cost Efficiency: By identifying scalability issues and optimizing resource allocation, organizations can avoid over-provisioning of resources, leading to cost savings in hardware, infrastructure, and maintenance.

5.4.6. Conclusion:

Virtualization and emulation technologies offer a powerful platform for network testing, enabling testers to create realistic and scalable environments for assessing functionality, performance, and security. Scalability testing, in particular, is crucial for ensuring that network infrastructure can handle increased workload and traffic volumes during peak periods. By leveraging virtualization and emulation tools, organizations can mitigate risks, optimize resource allocation, and improve the reliability and scalability of their network infrastructure.

CHAPTER 06

FUNCTIONAL TESTING

6.1. Verifying Network Services

Functional testing of network services involves validating the functionality and performance of various network devices and services, ensuring that they operate as intended and meet the specified requirements. This type of testing is crucial for ensuring the reliability, availability, and security of network infrastructure. Let's take an example of functional testing for network devices like switches.

Example: Functional Testing of Switches

Objective: Verify the functionality of a network switch by testing its basic operations, including port connectivity, VLAN configuration, and traffic forwarding.

Test Cases:

Port Connectivity Testing:

Test Scenario: Verify the connectivity of individual ports on the switch.

Test Steps:

Connect devices (e.g., PCs, servers) to each port on the switch.

Verify link status and connectivity for each port.

Expected Result: All ports should show a link status of "up," and devices connected to each port should be able to communicate with each other.

VLAN Configuration Testing:

Test Scenario: Validate the configuration of VLANs on the switch.

Test Steps:

Configure VLANs on the switch and assign ports to respective VLANs.

Verify VLAN membership and segregation by testing communication between devices in different VLANs.

Expected Result: Devices in the same VLAN should be able to communicate with each other, while communication between devices in different VLANs should be blocked.

Traffic Forwarding Testing:

Test Scenario: Ensure that the switch can forward traffic between connected devices efficiently.

Test Steps:

Generate traffic between devices connected to different ports on the switch.

Measure latency, throughput, and packet loss.

Expected Result: Traffic should be forwarded without significant latency or packet loss, and throughput should meet the specified requirements.

Spanning Tree Protocol (STP) Testing:

Test Scenario: Validate the operation of the Spanning Tree Protocol to prevent loops in the network.

Test Steps:

Introduce a redundant link between switches to create a potential loop.

Verify that STP blocks redundant links and prevents network loops.

Expected Result: STP should detect and block redundant links, ensuring network stability and preventing broadcast storms.

Quality of Service (QoS) Testing:

Test Scenario: Assess the switch's ability to prioritize traffic based on QoS policies.

Test Steps:

Configure QoS policies on the switch to prioritize specific types of traffic (e.g., VoIP).

Generate mixed traffic (e.g., VoIP, data) and measure latency and jitter for prioritized traffic.

Expected Result: Prioritized traffic should experience lower latency and jitter compared to non-prioritized traffic, meeting the defined QoS requirements.

Conclusion:

Functional testing of network devices like switches is essential for ensuring the reliability, performance, and security of network infrastructure. By systematically testing various aspects of switch functionality, including port connectivity, VLAN configuration, traffic forwarding, STP operation, and QoS policies, organizations can identify issues early in the deployment lifecycle and ensure that switches operate effectively in production environments. Effective functional testing helps mitigate risks, optimize network performance, and enhance the overall reliability of network services.

6.2. Validating Connectivity

Functional testing of network devices involves ensuring that connectivity is established and maintained as expected between various network elements. This type of testing verifies that devices can communicate with each other seamlessly and that network services are accessible. Let's consider an example of validating connectivity between network devices, specifically between a router and multiple client devices.

Example: Validating Connectivity between a Router and Client Devices

Objective: Verify that client devices can successfully establish connectivity with a router and access network services.

Test Cases:

I. **Basic Connectivity Test:**

   Test Scenario: Validate the ability of client devices to connect to the router.

   Test Steps:

   1. Configure the router with appropriate IP addressing and routing configurations.
   2. Connect client devices (e.g., PCs, laptops, smartphones) to the router's LAN ports.
   3. Verify that client devices receive IP addresses from the router's DHCP server.
   4. Attempt to ping the router's IP address from each client device.

   Expected Result: All client devices should successfully obtain IP addresses and be able to ping the router's IP address, indicating basic connectivity.

II. **Internet Connectivity Test:**

   Test Scenario: Ensure that client devices can access the internet through the router.

   Test Steps:

   1. Configure the router's WAN interface with appropriate internet connectivity settings (e.g., PPPoE, DHCP, static IP).
   2. Verify that the router obtains an IP address and DNS settings from the internet service provider (ISP).
   3. Attempt to ping external IP addresses (e.g., Google DNS servers) from client devices.
   4. Test web browsing and access to internet services (e.g., websites, online services) from client devices.

   Expected Result: Client devices should successfully ping external IP addresses and access internet services, indicating functional internet connectivity.

III. **LAN-to-LAN Connectivity Test:**

   Test Scenario: Validate connectivity between client devices on the LAN and devices on other LAN segments.

   Test Steps:

   1. Configure multiple VLANs on the router to segment the LAN.
   2. Connect client devices to different VLANs and configure appropriate IP addressing.
   3. Attempt to ping client devices in different VLANs and devices on other LAN segments (e.g., servers, printers).

   Expected Result: Client devices should be able to communicate with each other within the same VLAN and with devices on other LAN segments, demonstrating LAN-to-LAN connectivity.

IV. **Wireless Connectivity Test:**

Test Scenario: Verify connectivity for wireless client devices connecting to the router's wireless access point (WAP).

Test Steps:

1. Enable the wireless feature on the router and configure SSID, security settings, and encryption.
2. Connect wireless client devices (e.g., laptops, smartphones) to the router's wireless network.
3. Verify that wireless client devices obtain IP addresses and connect to the router's LAN.
4. Test ping connectivity and internet access for wireless client devices.

Expected Result: Wireless client devices should successfully connect to the router's wireless network, obtain IP addresses, and access network services, demonstrating functional wireless connectivity.

Conclusion:

Functional testing of connectivity between network devices is essential for ensuring the reliability and performance of network infrastructure. By systematically testing basic connectivity, internet connectivity, LAN-to-LAN connectivity, and wireless connectivity, organizations can verify that network devices function as expected and that client devices can access network services seamlessly. Effective functional testing helps identify connectivity issues early in the deployment lifecycle, ensuring that network services are accessible and reliable for end users.

6.3. Assessing Data Integrity

Functional testing of network devices involves ensuring that data transmitted over the network remains intact and unaltered during transmission. This type of testing verifies the integrity of data packets as they traverse network devices, such as routers, switches, and firewalls. Let's consider an example of assessing data integrity for network devices, focusing on the transmission of data packets between two routers.

Example: Assessing Data Integrity between Two Routers

Objective: Validate that data packets transmitted between two routers maintain integrity and are not corrupted or altered during transmission.

Test Cases:

I. **Basic Data Integrity Test:**

Test Scenario: Verify the integrity of data packets transmitted between two routers.

Test Steps:

1. Configure two routers with a direct physical or logical connection between them.
2. Generate a continuous stream of data packets from Router A to Router B using a traffic generation tool (e.g., ping utility, Iperf).
3. Capture and analyze the transmitted packets using a packet capture tool (e.g., Wireshark).

4. Verify that the captured packets arrive at Router B without any corruption or alteration.

Expected Result: All transmitted packets should arrive at Router B intact and unaltered, demonstrating data integrity.

II. Packet Loss Test:

Test Scenario: Assess the impact of network congestion or packet loss on data integrity.

Test Steps:

1. Introduce network congestion or packet loss between Router A and Router B by simulating high traffic or network conditions.
2. Generate a stream of data packets from Router A to Router B under congested or lossy conditions.
3. Capture and analyze the transmitted packets to identify any instances of packet loss or corruption.

Expected Result: While some packets may be lost or corrupted under congested or lossy conditions, the majority of transmitted packets should arrive at Router B intact.

III. Error Detection and Correction Test:

Test Scenario: Evaluate the error detection and correction mechanisms implemented in network devices.

Test Steps:

1. Configure Router A to transmit data packets with intentional errors (e.g., checksum errors, sequence number errors).
2. Capture and analyze the transmitted packets at Router B to identify any detected errors or correction attempts.
3. Verify that Router B correctly detects and, if applicable, corrects errors in received packets.

Expected Result: Router B should detect and, if supported, correct any errors in received packets, ensuring data integrity is maintained.

IV. Security Testing for Data Integrity:

Test Scenario: Assess the impact of security mechanisms (e.g., encryption, authentication) on data integrity.

Test Steps:

1. Configure Router A and Router B with encrypted communication using a secure protocol (e.g., IPsec, SSL/TLS).
2. Generate encrypted data packets from Router A to Router B and capture them at Router B.
3. Decrypt and analyze the received packets to ensure that data integrity is preserved even with encryption.

Expected Result: Encrypted data packets should maintain integrity during transmission and decryption, demonstrating the effectiveness of security measures in preserving data integrity.

Conclusion:

Functional testing of data integrity for network devices is crucial for ensuring the reliability and security of data transmitted over the network. By systematically testing data integrity under various conditions, including normal operation, network congestion, error conditions, and encrypted communication, organizations can verify that network devices maintain the integrity of transmitted data packets. Effective functional testing helps identify potential issues with data integrity early in the deployment lifecycle, ensuring that data remains intact and unaltered as it traverses network infrastructure.

In addition to verifying network services, validating connectivity, and assessing data integrity, there are several other areas that can be covered in functional testing for network devices. Here are a few additional aspects to consider:

V. Protocol Conformance Testing:
- Ensure that network devices adhere to industry-standard protocols (e.g., TCP/IP, UDP, ICMP) and comply with protocol specifications.
- Validate protocol implementations for correctness, interoperability, and compliance with relevant RFCs (Request for Comments).

VI. Configuration Management Testing:
- Verify the functionality of configuration management features, such as backup and restore, configuration versioning, and rollback.
- Test the ability to push configuration changes to multiple devices simultaneously and ensure consistency across the network.

VII. High Availability and Redundancy Testing:
- Assess the failover mechanisms and redundancy features of network devices, such as hot standby, VRRP (Virtual Router Redundancy Protocol), and HSRP (Hot Standby Router Protocol).
- Validate the behavior of network devices during failover events and ensure uninterrupted service availability.

VIII. Load Balancing and Traffic Management Testing:
- Evaluate the effectiveness of load balancing algorithms and traffic management policies implemented in network devices, such as QoS (Quality of Service) policies, traffic shaping, and prioritization.
- Test the ability of devices to handle and distribute network traffic efficiently under varying load conditions.

IX. Routing and Switching Functionality Testing:
- Validate routing protocols (e.g., OSPF, BGP, EIGRP) and switching functionalities (e.g., VLAN trunking, Spanning Tree Protocol) to ensure proper routing and switching behavior.
- Test dynamic routing updates, route convergence, and loop prevention mechanisms.

X. Interoperability Testing:

- Ensure interoperability between different vendor devices and software versions by testing compatibility and adherence to industry standards.
- Validate interoperability with third-party devices and systems, such as firewalls, load balancers, and network management systems.

XI. Performance Benchmarking:

- Measure the performance metrics of network devices, including throughput, latency, packet loss, and CPU/memory utilization.
- Conduct stress testing and scalability testing to assess the performance limits of network devices and identify potential bottlenecks.

XII. Logging and Monitoring Testing:

- Verify the functionality of logging and monitoring features, such as syslog, SNMP (Simple Network Management Protocol), and NetFlow.
- Test the generation, storage, and retrieval of log messages and monitoring data for troubleshooting and analysis purposes.

XIII. Security Functionality Testing:

- Assess the security features and capabilities of network devices, including access control lists (ACLs), firewall policies, VPN (Virtual Private Network) configurations, and intrusion detection/prevention systems.
- Test for vulnerabilities, misconfigurations, and compliance with security best practices and regulatory requirements.

By covering these additional areas in functional testing, organizations can ensure the reliability, performance, security, and interoperability of their network infrastructure. Effective functional testing helps identify and address issues early in the deployment lifecycle, reducing the risk of service disruptions and ensuring the smooth operation of network services.

PERFORMANCE TESTING

CHAPTER 07

7.1. Bandwidth Testing

Performance testing of network devices involves assessing their ability to handle and sustain data transfer rates, commonly referred to as bandwidth. Bandwidth testing is essential for ensuring that network devices can meet the required throughput and performance demands of applications and services. Let's explore an example of bandwidth testing for network devices, focusing on a router.

Example: Bandwidth Testing for a Router

Objective: Measure the maximum achievable bandwidth of a router under different network conditions to ensure it meets performance requirements.

Test Setup:

Network Topology: A simple network topology consisting of a router connected to a source device (e.g., PC) and a destination device (e.g., server). Refer to Fig-9.1.1: Device and Platform Compatibility diagram

Test Tools: Iperf or similar network performance testing tools for generating traffic and measuring bandwidth.

Test Cases:

I. **Baseline Bandwidth Test:**

Test Scenario: Measure the baseline bandwidth between the source and destination devices through the router under normal operating conditions.

Test Steps:

1. Configure the source and destination devices with static IP addresses.
2. Use Iperf to generate TCP or UDP traffic between the source and destination devices through the router.
3. Measure the bandwidth using Iperf's reporting feature.

Expected Result: Obtain baseline bandwidth metrics (e.g., throughput in Mbps or Gbps) reflecting the router's normal performance.

II. Throughput Testing:

Test Scenario: Assess the router's throughput capabilities under varying traffic loads.

Test Steps:

1. Gradually increase the traffic load using Iperf to simulate different levels of network utilization.
2. Measure the bandwidth at each traffic load increment to determine the router's throughput capacity.

Expected Result: Identify the maximum sustainable throughput of the router under different load conditions and ensure it meets performance requirements.

III. Bidirectional Bandwidth Test:

Test Scenario: Evaluate the router's bidirectional bandwidth capabilities for simultaneous upload and download traffic.

Test Steps:

1. Configure Iperf to generate bidirectional traffic between the source and destination devices simultaneously.
2. Measure the upload and download bandwidth separately and collectively.

Expected Result: Ensure that the router can handle bidirectional traffic efficiently without significant degradation in performance.

IV. Quality of Service (QoS) Testing:

Test Scenario: Validate the router's ability to prioritize traffic and maintain performance for high-priority applications.

Test Steps:

1. Configure QoS policies on the router to prioritize specific types of traffic (e.g., VoIP, video streaming).
2. Generate mixed traffic with different QoS priorities using Iperf and measure the bandwidth for each traffic category.

Expected Result: Verify that high-priority traffic receives adequate bandwidth allocation and does not suffer from performance degradation due to lower-priority traffic.

Conclusion:

Bandwidth testing is crucial for evaluating the performance capabilities of network devices, such as routers, and ensuring they can meet the demands of modern networking environments. By conducting bandwidth testing under various conditions and scenarios, organizations can identify performance bottlenecks, optimize network configurations, and ensure that network devices can deliver the required throughput for applications and services. Effective bandwidth testing helps maintain optimal network performance and user experience, contributing to the overall reliability and efficiency of the network infrastructure.

7.2. Latency and Packet Loss Analysis

Performance testing of network devices involves evaluating their ability to transmit data efficiently, without significant delays (latency) and packet loss. Latency and packet loss analysis is crucial for assessing the responsiveness and reliability of network communication. Let's delve into an example of latency and packet loss analysis for network devices, focusing on a network switch.

Example: Latency and Packet Loss Analysis for a Network Switch

Objective: Measure the latency and packet loss introduced by a network switch under varying network conditions to ensure optimal performance.

Test Setup:

Network Topology: A simple network topology consisting of a network switch connected to multiple client devices (e.g., PCs, servers). Refer to Fig-9.1.1: Device and Platform Compatibility diagram

Test Tools: Ping utility for latency measurement and packet loss detection.

Test Cases:

I. **Baseline Latency Test:**

Test Scenario: Measure the baseline latency introduced by the network switch under normal operating conditions.

Test Steps:

1. Ping a client device connected to the switch from another client device.
2. Measure the round-trip time (RTT) of ICMP (Internet Control Message Protocol) echo requests and responses.

Expected Result: Obtain baseline latency metrics reflecting the switch's normal performance.

II. **Latency Variation Test:**

Test Scenario: Assess how latency varies under different network loads and conditions.

Test Steps:

1. Generate varying levels of network traffic using bandwidth-intensive applications or traffic generation tools.
2. Continuously ping client devices connected to the switch and monitor latency fluctuations.

Expected Result: Identify how latency changes as network utilization increases or decreases, and ensure it remains within acceptable limits.

III. **Jitter Analysis:**

Test Scenario: Evaluate the variability (jitter) in latency introduced by the network switch.

Test Steps:

1. Ping a client device at regular intervals (e.g., every second) over an extended period.

2. Calculate the difference between successive RTT measurements to determine jitter.

Expected Result: Assess the consistency of latency over time and quantify the level of jitter experienced by network traffic.

IV. **Packet Loss Testing:**

Test Scenario: Measure the rate of packet loss introduced by the network switch.

Test Steps:

1. Continuously ping a client device from another client device connected to the switch.
2. Monitor the percentage of ICMP echo requests that do not receive corresponding responses.

Expected Result: Determine the percentage of packet loss experienced by network traffic and ensure it remains within acceptable thresholds.

V. **Quality of Service (QoS) Analysis:**

Test Scenario: Validate the effectiveness of QoS mechanisms in minimizing latency and packet loss for high-priority traffic.

Test Steps:

1. Configure QoS policies on the switch to prioritize specific types of traffic (e.g., VoIP, video streaming).
2. Generate mixed traffic with different QoS priorities and measure latency and packet loss for each traffic category.

Expected Result: Verify that high-priority traffic receives preferential treatment and experiences lower latency and packet loss compared to lower-priority traffic.

Conclusion:

Latency and packet loss analysis are essential components of performance testing for network devices, such as switches, as they directly impact the responsiveness and reliability of network communication. By conducting comprehensive latency and packet loss analysis under various network conditions, organizations can identify potential performance issues, optimize network configurations, and ensure optimal network performance. Effective analysis of latency, jitter, and packet loss helps maintain a high-quality user experience and ensures the efficient operation of network infrastructure.

7.3. Scalability Testing

Scalability testing for network devices involves assessing their ability to handle increasing workload and traffic volumes while maintaining optimal performance and reliability. This type of testing is crucial for ensuring that network devices can scale effectively to accommodate growing demands in real-world scenarios. Let's explore an example of scalability testing for network devices, focusing on a network firewall.

Example: Scalability Testing for a Network Firewall

Objective: Evaluate the scalability of a network firewall by assessing its performance under increasing traffic loads and connections.

Test Setup:

Network Topology: A network topology comprising multiple client devices (e.g., PCs, servers) accessing the internet through the firewall. Refer to Fig-9.1.1: Device and Platform Compatibility diagram

Test Tools: Traffic generation tools (e.g., Iperf, DDoS simulators) for generating network traffic, monitoring tools for performance metrics.

Test Cases:

I. Baseline Performance Test:

Test Scenario: Measure the baseline performance of the firewall under normal operating conditions with a typical network load.

Test Steps:

1. Configure the firewall with standard traffic filtering rules and policies.
2. Generate a steady stream of network traffic from client devices to external destinations.
3. Monitor the firewall's performance metrics, including CPU and memory utilization, throughput, latency, and connection count.

Expected Result: Obtain baseline performance metrics to establish a reference point for scalability testing.

II. Traffic Load Testing:

Test Scenario: Assess the firewall's ability to handle increasing traffic loads while maintaining performance.

Test Steps:

1. Gradually increase the amount of network traffic directed through the firewall by increasing the number of client devices or generating additional traffic.
2. Continuously monitor the firewall's performance metrics under increasing traffic loads, including throughput, latency, and resource utilization.

Expected Result: Identify the maximum sustainable traffic load that the firewall can handle while maintaining acceptable performance levels.

III. Connection Capacity Testing:

Test Scenario: Evaluate the firewall's capacity to handle a large number of simultaneous connections.

Test Steps:

1. Establish a baseline number of concurrent connections and gradually increase the number of simultaneous connections.

2. Monitor the firewall's performance metrics, including connection count, CPU and memory utilization, and throughput.

Expected Result: Determine the maximum number of concurrent connections that the firewall can support without experiencing performance degradation or resource exhaustion.

IV. Security Policy Complexity Testing:

Test Scenario: Assess the impact of complex security policies and rule sets on firewall performance.

Test Steps:

1. Configure the firewall with complex security policies, including advanced filtering rules, application-layer inspection, and deep packet inspection.

2. Generate network traffic that matches the criteria defined by the security policies and measure the firewall's performance.

Expected Result: Evaluate how the complexity of security policies affects the firewall's performance and scalability, identifying any bottlenecks or limitations.

Conclusion:

Scalability testing for network devices, such as firewalls, is essential for ensuring that they can effectively handle increasing traffic loads and connection volumes without compromising performance or reliability. By systematically testing scalability under various conditions, organizations can identify performance bottlenecks, optimize configurations, and ensure that network devices can scale to meet the demands of growing network environments. Effective scalability testing helps maintain optimal network performance, minimize downtime, and ensure a high-quality user experience.

7.4. Throughput and Capacity Planning

Throughput and capacity planning testing for network devices involve assessing their ability to handle data transfer rates and determining the maximum capacity they can support under various conditions. This type of testing is essential for ensuring that network devices can meet the bandwidth requirements of applications and services while maintaining optimal performance. Let's explore an example of throughput and capacity planning testing for network devices, focusing on a network switch.

Example: Throughput and Capacity Planning Testing for a Network Switch

Objective: Measure the throughput capabilities and determine the maximum capacity of a network switch under different traffic loads.

Test Setup:

Network Topology: A network topology comprising the network switch connected to multiple client devices (e.g., PCs, servers). Refer to Fig-9.1.1: Device and Platform Compatibility diagram

Test Tools: Traffic generation tools (e.g., Iperf, Jperf) for generating network traffic, monitoring tools for performance metrics.

Test Cases:

I. **Baseline Throughput Test:**

   Test Scenario: Measure the baseline throughput of the network switch under normal operating conditions.

   Test Steps:

   1. Configure the network switch with standard port configurations and traffic filtering settings.
   2. Generate a steady stream of network traffic between client devices connected to different ports of the switch.
   3. Measure the throughput using traffic generation tools and monitor performance metrics such as data transfer rate (Mbps or Gbps).

   Expected Result: Obtain baseline throughput metrics representing the switch's normal performance.

II. **Throughput Variation Test:**

   Test Scenario: Assess how throughput varies under different traffic loads and conditions.

   Test Steps:

   1. Gradually increase the amount of network traffic directed through the switch by increasing the number of client devices or generating additional traffic.
   2. Continuously monitor the switch's performance metrics, including throughput and packet loss, under varying traffic loads.

   Expected Result: Identify how throughput changes as network utilization increases or decreases, ensuring it remains within acceptable limits.

III. **Maximum Throughput Test:**

   Test Scenario: Determine the maximum achievable throughput of the network switch under optimal conditions.

   Test Steps:

   1. Configure the network switch with optimized settings and configurations to maximize performance.
   2. Generate a high volume of network traffic to saturate the switch's capacity.
   3. Measure the maximum throughput achieved by the switch and ensure it meets performance requirements.

   Expected Result: Determine the maximum data transfer rate supported by the switch without experiencing performance degradation or packet loss.

IV. Capacity Planning Analysis:

Test Scenario: Estimate the switch's capacity and plan for future network expansion based on throughput measurements.

Test Steps:

1. Analyze the switch's performance metrics, including throughput, latency, and resource utilization, under different traffic loads.
2. Project future network growth and calculate the expected increase in traffic volume.
3. Determine whether the switch can accommodate future network demands or if additional capacity or upgrades are necessary.

Expected Result: Provide recommendations for capacity planning based on the switch's throughput capabilities and anticipated network growth.

In addition to bandwidth testing, latency and packet loss analysis, scalability testing, and throughput and capacity planning, there are several other areas that can be covered in performance testing for network devices. Here are a few additional aspects to consider:

V. Quality of Service (QoS) Testing:

- Evaluate the effectiveness of QoS mechanisms in prioritizing and managing network traffic according to predefined policies.
- Test QoS parameters such as packet prioritization, bandwidth allocation, and traffic shaping under different traffic conditions.

VI. Load Balancing Testing:

- Assess the load balancing capabilities of network devices, such as routers and load balancers, in distributing traffic across multiple paths or servers.
- Test load balancing algorithms, failover mechanisms, and session persistence under varying loads and failure scenarios.

VII. Buffer and Queue Management Testing:

- Evaluate the buffer and queue management mechanisms implemented in network devices to handle incoming and outgoing traffic.
- Test buffer sizes, queueing algorithms, and congestion control mechanisms to ensure optimal performance and minimize packet loss.

VIII. Routing Protocol Performance Testing:

- Assess the performance of routing protocols (e.g., OSPF, BGP) in dynamically updating routing tables and determining optimal paths.
- Test route convergence times, route flapping behavior, and scalability of routing protocols in large-scale networks.

IX. Multicast and Broadcast Testing:

- Evaluate the performance of multicast and broadcast traffic handling in network devices, such as switches and routers.
- Test multicast group communication, IGMP (Internet Group Management Protocol) behavior, and multicast replication efficiency.

X. High Availability and Redundancy Testing:

- Assess the failover and redundancy mechanisms implemented in network devices to ensure continuous operation in the event of failures.
- Test failover times, failback behavior, and failover testing with redundant links, devices, and protocols.

XI. Protocol Interoperability Testing:

- Validate the interoperability of network devices with different vendor equipment and software versions.
- Test protocol compatibility, standards compliance, and interoperability with third-party devices and systems.

XII. Security Performance Testing:

- Evaluate the performance impact of security features such as encryption, authentication, and intrusion prevention systems (IPS).
- Test the throughput, latency, and resource utilization of network devices with enabled security features under normal and attack conditions.

Conclusion:

Throughput and capacity planning testing for network devices, such as switches, is essential for ensuring that they can effectively handle data transfer rates and meet the bandwidth requirements of applications and services. By systematically testing throughput and capacity under various conditions, organizations can identify performance limitations, optimize configurations, and plan for future network expansion. Effective throughput and capacity planning testing help ensure that network devices can scale to meet the demands of growing network environments and maintain optimal performance and reliability.

By covering these additional areas in performance testing, organizations can ensure the reliability, scalability, and optimal performance of their network infrastructure. Effective performance testing helps identify potential issues, optimize configurations, and ensure that network devices can meet the demands of modern networking environments.

CHAPTER 08

SECURITY TESTING

8.1. Vulnerability Assessment

Vulnerability assessment is a critical aspect of security testing for network devices, aiming to identify and mitigate potential security vulnerabilities that could be exploited by attackers. This process involves systematically scanning network devices for known vulnerabilities and weaknesses to assess their security posture. Let's explore an example of vulnerability assessment for network devices, focusing on a network firewall.

Example: Vulnerability Assessment for a Network Firewall

Objective: Identify and mitigate potential security vulnerabilities in a network firewall to enhance its resilience against cyber threats.

Test Setup:

Network Topology: A network topology comprising the network firewall deployed between the internal network and the internet.

Test Tools: Vulnerability scanning tools (e.g., Nessus, OpenVAS) for identifying security vulnerabilities, network sniffers for capturing network traffic.

Test Cases:

I. **Vulnerability Scan:**

Test Scenario: Conduct an automated vulnerability scan of the network firewall to identify known security vulnerabilities.

Test Steps:

1. Configure the vulnerability scanning tool to perform a comprehensive scan of the firewall's configuration and services.
2. Initiate the vulnerability scan and analyze the results to identify potential vulnerabilities, misconfigurations, and weaknesses.

Expected Result: Generate a report detailing the vulnerabilities discovered during the scan, including severity ratings and recommended remediation steps.

II. Configuration Audit:

Test Scenario: Perform a manual audit of the firewall's configuration settings to identify insecure or non-compliant configurations.

Test Steps:

1. Review the firewall's configuration settings, including access control rules, firewall policies, and security settings.
2. Identify any configuration errors, deprecated protocols, or insecure settings that could pose security risks.

Expected Result: Document findings from the configuration audit and provide recommendations for addressing identified security issues through configuration changes.

III. Patch Management Assessment:

Test Scenario: Evaluate the effectiveness of patch management practices for the firewall in addressing known security vulnerabilities.

Test Steps:

1. Verify the current patch level of the firewall's operating system and firmware/software components.
2. Cross-reference the patch level against known security vulnerabilities and missing patches.

Expected Result: Identify any missing patches or outdated software versions that may expose the firewall to known security vulnerabilities and recommend patching or updating as necessary.

IV. Traffic Analysis for Anomaly Detection:

Test Scenario: Monitor network traffic passing through the firewall to detect suspicious or malicious activity indicative of potential security breaches.

Test Steps:

1. Deploy network sniffers or intrusion detection systems (IDS) to monitor inbound and outbound traffic flows.
2. Analyze network traffic patterns, anomalies, and security events to identify potential security threats or unauthorized activities.

Expected Result: Detect and investigate any anomalies or security events detected during traffic analysis, such as unusual network traffic patterns or unauthorized access attempts.

Conclusion:

Vulnerability assessment for network devices, such as firewalls, is crucial for identifying and mitigating potential security risks that could compromise the confidentiality, integrity, and availability of network resources. By systematically scanning for vulnerabilities, auditing configurations, assessing patch management practices, and monitoring network traffic, organizations can enhance the security posture of their network infrastructure and minimize the risk of cyber attacks. Effective vulnerability assessment helps proactively identify and address security vulnerabilities before they can be exploited by malicious actors, thereby strengthening the overall security resilience of the network environment.

8.2. Penetration Testing

Penetration testing, also known as ethical hacking, is a proactive security testing technique that involves simulating real-world cyber attacks to identify vulnerabilities in network devices and assess the effectiveness of security controls. This process aims to uncover potential security weaknesses that could be exploited by attackers and provides insights into the organization's overall security posture. Let's explore an example of penetration testing for network devices, focusing on a network router.

Example: Penetration Testing for a Network Router

Objective: Assess the security resilience of a network router by simulating various cyber attacks to identify potential vulnerabilities and weaknesses.

Test Setup:

Network Topology: A network topology comprising the network router serving as the gateway between the internal network and the internet.

Test Tools: Penetration testing tools (e.g., Metasploit, Nmap), network sniffers, exploit frameworks.

Test Cases:

I. **Network Enumeration:**

Test Scenario: Perform network reconnaissance to gather information about the network topology, devices, and services.

Test Steps:

1. Use network scanning tools such as Nmap to discover active hosts and open ports on the network.
2. Enumerate network services and identify potential targets, including the network router.

Expected Result: Compile a network map detailing the topology and identify potential entry points for further exploitation.

II. **Vulnerability Scanning:**

Test Scenario: Conduct vulnerability scanning of the network router to identify known security vulnerabilities.

Test Steps:

1. Utilize vulnerability scanning tools such as Nessus or OpenVAS to scan the network router for known vulnerabilities.
2. Analyze the scan results to identify exploitable vulnerabilities, misconfigurations, and weaknesses.

Expected Result: Generate a report listing identified vulnerabilities with severity ratings and recommended remediation steps.

III. Exploitation Attempts:

Test Scenario: Attempt to exploit identified vulnerabilities on the network router to gain unauthorized access or control.

Test Steps:

1. Use penetration testing tools such as Metasploit to launch exploit attempts targeting known vulnerabilities.
2. Attempt to exploit vulnerabilities in the router's firmware, software, or configuration settings.

Expected Result: Successfully exploit vulnerabilities to demonstrate potential security risks and the impact of successful attacks.

IV. Privilege Escalation:

Test Scenario: Attempt to escalate privileges on the network router to gain higher levels of access and control.

Test Steps:

1. Exploit vulnerabilities to gain initial access to the router and establish a foothold.
2. Attempt to escalate privileges by exploiting misconfigurations or weaknesses in access control mechanisms.

Expected Result: Gain elevated privileges on the router, demonstrating the potential for unauthorized access and control.

V. Post-Exploitation Activities:

Test Scenario: Perform post-exploitation activities to demonstrate the impact of a successful compromise.

Test Steps:

1. Maintain persistence on the compromised router by establishing backdoors or creating user accounts.
2. Conduct reconnaissance to gather sensitive information or attempt to pivot to other network devices.

Expected Result: Demonstrate the potential consequences of a successful attack, such as data exfiltration, network reconnaissance, or unauthorized access to critical systems.

Conclusion:

Penetration testing for network devices, such as routers, is an essential component of cybersecurity testing strategies, helping organizations identify and mitigate potential security risks before they can be exploited by malicious actors. By simulating real-world cyber attacks and attempting to exploit vulnerabilities, penetration testing provides valuable insights into the effectiveness of security controls and helps organizations strengthen their overall security posture. Effective penetration testing helps identify and remediate security vulnerabilities, reduce the risk of data breaches and cyber attacks, and enhance the resilience of network infrastructure against emerging threats.

8.3. Firewall and Intrusion Detection System Testing

Firewalls and Intrusion Detection Systems (IDS) are critical components of network security infrastructure, responsible for monitoring and controlling network traffic to protect against unauthorized access, malicious activities, and cyber threats. Security testing for firewalls and IDS involves assessing their effectiveness in filtering, detecting, and responding to security incidents. Let's explore an example of firewall and IDS testing, focusing on a network environment protected by a firewall and IDS.

Example: Firewall and Intrusion Detection System (IDS) Testing

Objective: Evaluate the performance and effectiveness of a firewall and IDS in protecting the network against unauthorized access, malicious activities, and cyber threats.

Test Setup:

Network Topology: A network topology comprising client devices, servers, a firewall deployed at the network perimeter, and an IDS positioned to monitor network traffic.

Test Tools: Network scanning tools (e.g., Nmap), traffic generation tools (e.g., Hping), IDS evasion tools (e.g., SnortSam), penetration testing frameworks (e.g., Metasploit).

Test Cases:

I. **Firewall Rule Assessment:**

Test Scenario: Review and assess the firewall's access control rules, policies, and configurations to ensure they align with security best practices and organizational policies.

Test Steps:

1. Review the firewall's ruleset to identify allowed and denied traffic, NAT (Network Address Translation) configurations, and application-layer filtering rules.

2. Evaluate the effectiveness of the firewall's rule set in preventing unauthorized access and mitigating common attack vectors.

Expected Result: Identify any misconfigurations, overly permissive rules, or gaps in firewall policies that could potentially expose the network to security risks.

II. **Firewall Evasion Testing:**

Test Scenario: Attempt to bypass or evade the firewall's security mechanisms to gain unauthorized access to the network.

Test Steps:

1. Use network scanning tools such as Nmap to identify open ports and services on the network.
2. Attempt to exploit vulnerabilities or weaknesses in the firewall's rule set to circumvent access restrictions and penetrate the network perimeter.

Expected Result: Demonstrate the effectiveness of the firewall in detecting and blocking evasion attempts, or identify vulnerabilities that need to be addressed.

III. Intrusion Detection System (IDS) Evaluation:

Test Scenario: Assess the IDS's ability to detect and respond to security threats and anomalous activities on the network.

Test Steps:

1. Generate simulated attack traffic or malicious activities on the network, such as port scans, denial-of-service (DoS) attacks, or SQL injection attempts.
2. Monitor the IDS's alerts and notifications to evaluate its ability to detect and alert on suspicious network behavior.

Expected Result: Validate the IDS's effectiveness in detecting known threats and anomalous activities, as well as its ability to generate accurate and timely alerts.

IV. False Positive and False Negative Analysis:

Test Scenario: Evaluate the IDS's performance in minimizing false positive and false negative alerts to ensure accurate threat detection.

Test Steps:

1. Generate benign and malicious network traffic to trigger alerts from the IDS.
2. Analyze the IDS's alerts to assess the rate of false positives (incorrectly identifying benign traffic as malicious) and false negatives (failing to detect actual threats).

Expected Result: Minimize false positives to reduce alert fatigue and prioritize accurate threat detection to minimize the risk of undetected security incidents.

V. Performance and Scalability Testing:

Test Scenario: Assess the performance and scalability of the firewall and IDS under normal and peak traffic loads.

Test Steps:

1. Generate varying levels of network traffic to simulate different usage scenarios and stress the firewall and IDS.

2. Monitor the performance metrics of the firewall and IDS, including CPU and memory utilization, throughput, and latency.

Expected Result: Ensure that the firewall and IDS can handle expected traffic volumes without degradation in performance or dropped packets.

Conclusion:

Firewall and Intrusion Detection System (IDS) testing is essential for evaluating the effectiveness of network security controls in protecting against unauthorized access, malicious activities, and cyber threats. By systematically assessing firewall rules, conducting evasion testing, evaluating IDS alerts, and analyzing performance and scalability, organizations can identify potential security weaknesses, optimize configurations, and enhance the overall security posture of their network infrastructure. Effective testing helps ensure that firewalls and IDSs can detect and respond to security threats in a timely and efficient manner, thereby reducing the risk of security breaches and data loss.

8.4. SSL/TLS Testing

SSL/TLS (Secure Sockets Layer/Transport Layer Security) protocols are fundamental to securing communication over computer networks. SSL/TLS testing involves assessing the implementation and configuration of SSL/TLS protocols on network devices, such as web servers, to ensure they adhere to security best practices and mitigate vulnerabilities. Let's explore an example of SSL/TLS testing for network devices, focusing on a web server.

Example: SSL/TLS Testing for a Web Server

Objective: Evaluate the SSL/TLS implementation and configuration of a web server to identify potential security vulnerabilities and ensure compliance with security standards.

Test Setup:

Network Topology: A network topology comprising a web server hosting HTTPS-enabled websites.

Test Tools: SSL/TLS testing tools (e.g., SSL Labs, OpenSSL), network sniffers (e.g., Wireshark), vulnerability scanners (e.g., Nessus).

Test Cases:

I. **SSL/TLS Protocol Version Support:**

Test Scenario: Evaluate the web server's support for SSL/TLS protocol versions and assess the security implications of supported versions.

Test Steps:

1. Use SSL/TLS testing tools to assess which versions of SSL/TLS are supported by the web server.
2. Analyze the security implications of supported protocol versions, such as susceptibility to known vulnerabilities (e.g., POODLE, BEAST).

Expected Result: Ensure that the web server supports secure SSL/TLS protocol versions (e.g., TLS 1.2 or later) and mitigates known vulnerabilities associated with deprecated versions.

II. SSL/TLS Certificate Configuration:

Test Scenario: Verify the correctness and validity of SSL/TLS certificates used by the web server to establish secure connections.

Test Steps:

1. Inspect the SSL/TLS certificates installed on the web server, including server certificates, intermediate certificates, and root certificates.
2. Validate the certificates for correct issuance, expiration dates, and compliance with industry standards (e.g., X.509).

Expected Result: Ensure that SSL/TLS certificates are correctly configured, valid, and issued by trusted Certificate Authorities (CAs) to establish secure connections without warnings or errors.

III. Cipher Suite Configuration:

Test Scenario: Assess the strength and security of SSL/TLS cipher suites configured on the web server to secure communications.

Test Steps:

1. Review the web server's SSL/TLS cipher suite configuration to ensure it includes strong, secure cipher suites.
2. Evaluate the resilience of configured cipher suites against known vulnerabilities and attacks (e.g., CBC attacks, weak key exchange algorithms).

Expected Result: Configure the web server to prioritize secure cipher suites with strong encryption algorithms, perfect forward secrecy (PFS), and resistance to cryptographic attacks.

IV. SSL/TLS Handshake Analysis:

Test Scenario: Analyze the SSL/TLS handshake process between clients and the web server to ensure secure and efficient communication.

Test Steps:

1. Capture and analyze network traffic using network sniffers to inspect SSL/TLS handshake messages exchanged during connection establishment.
2. Evaluate the SSL/TLS handshake for adherence to best practices, proper certificate validation, and negotiation of secure parameters.

Expected Result: Confirm that the SSL/TLS handshake process follows security best practices and establishes secure connections with clients without vulnerabilities or weaknesses.

V. SSL/TLS Vulnerability Scanning:

Test Scenario: Conduct vulnerability scanning of the web server's SSL/TLS configuration to identify potential security vulnerabilities.

Test Steps:

1. Utilize SSL/TLS testing tools or vulnerability scanners to perform automated scans of the web server's SSL/TLS configuration.

2. Analyze scan results to identify misconfigurations, weaknesses, or vulnerabilities in SSL/TLS settings.

Expected Result: Address identified vulnerabilities and weaknesses in the SSL/TLS configuration to mitigate potential security risks and ensure compliance with security standards.

Conclusion:

SSL/TLS testing for network devices, such as web servers, is essential for ensuring secure communication and protecting sensitive data transmitted over computer networks. By evaluating SSL/TLS protocol support, certificate configuration, cipher suite selection, handshake process, and vulnerability scanning, organizations can identify and mitigate potential security vulnerabilities, strengthen the security posture of their web servers, and enhance overall network security. Effective SSL/TLS testing helps ensure that web servers adhere to industry best practices and standards, providing secure and trustworthy communication channels for users accessing web-based services and applications.

In addition to vulnerability assessment, penetration testing, firewall and intrusion detection system (IDS) testing, and SSL/TLS testing, there are several other areas that can be covered in security testing for network devices. Here are a few additional aspects to consider:

VI. Access Control Testing:

- Evaluate the effectiveness of access control mechanisms implemented on network devices, such as routers, switches, and firewalls.
- Test user authentication mechanisms, privilege escalation controls, and role-based access policies to ensure proper enforcement of access rights.

VII. Data Encryption Testing:

- Assess the implementation and strength of data encryption mechanisms used to protect sensitive information transmitted over the network.
- Test encryption protocols, key management practices, and data encryption at rest and in transit to ensure data confidentiality and integrity.

VIII. Security Configuration Review:

- Review the security configuration settings of network devices to identify potential misconfigurations, insecure defaults, and weak security settings.

- Assess configurations related to network services, access controls, logging and auditing, and security policies for adherence to security best practices.

IX. Denial of Service (DoS) Testing:

- Evaluate the resilience of network devices against denial-of-service (DoS) attacks aimed at disrupting or degrading network services.
- Test network devices' ability to detect, mitigate, and recover from DoS attacks, including volumetric attacks, protocol attacks, and application-layer attacks.

X. Web Application Security Testing:

- Assess the security of web applications hosted on network devices, such as web servers and application servers.
- Test for common web application vulnerabilities, such as SQL injection, cross-site scripting (XSS), and insecure direct object references (IDOR).

XI. Wireless Security Testing:

- Evaluate the security of wireless networks and wireless access points (WAPs) to identify vulnerabilities and weaknesses.
- Test for weaknesses in Wi-Fi encryption (e.g., WEP, WPA2), authentication mechanisms, and rogue access point detection.

XII. Physical Security Assessment:

- Assess the physical security measures implemented to protect network devices from unauthorized access, tampering, and theft.
- Test physical access controls, surveillance systems, and environmental controls (e.g., temperature, humidity) to ensure the integrity and availability of network infrastructure.

XIII. Social Engineering Testing:

- Evaluate the effectiveness of security awareness training and measures to mitigate social engineering attacks targeting network users and administrators.
- Test user awareness, susceptibility to phishing attacks, and responses to social engineering tactics aimed at extracting sensitive information or gaining unauthorized access.

By covering these additional areas in security testing, organizations can comprehensively assess the security posture of their network infrastructure and identify potential vulnerabilities, weaknesses, and areas for improvement. Effective security testing helps mitigate security risks, protect against cyber threats, and ensure the confidentiality, integrity, and availability of network resources and data.

CHAPTER 09

COMPATIBILITY TESTING

9.1. Device and Platform Compatibility

Compatibility testing ensures that network devices and platforms work seamlessly together, regardless of their configurations or specifications. This testing verifies that network devices, such as routers, switches, firewalls, and access points, are compatible with various hardware, software, and operating systems to ensure interoperability and optimal performance. Let's explore an example of compatibility testing for network devices, focusing on router and switch compatibility.

Example: Device and Platform Compatibility Testing for Network Devices

Objective: Validate the compatibility of routers and switches with different hardware, software, and operating systems to ensure seamless integration and interoperability in diverse network environments.

Test Setup:

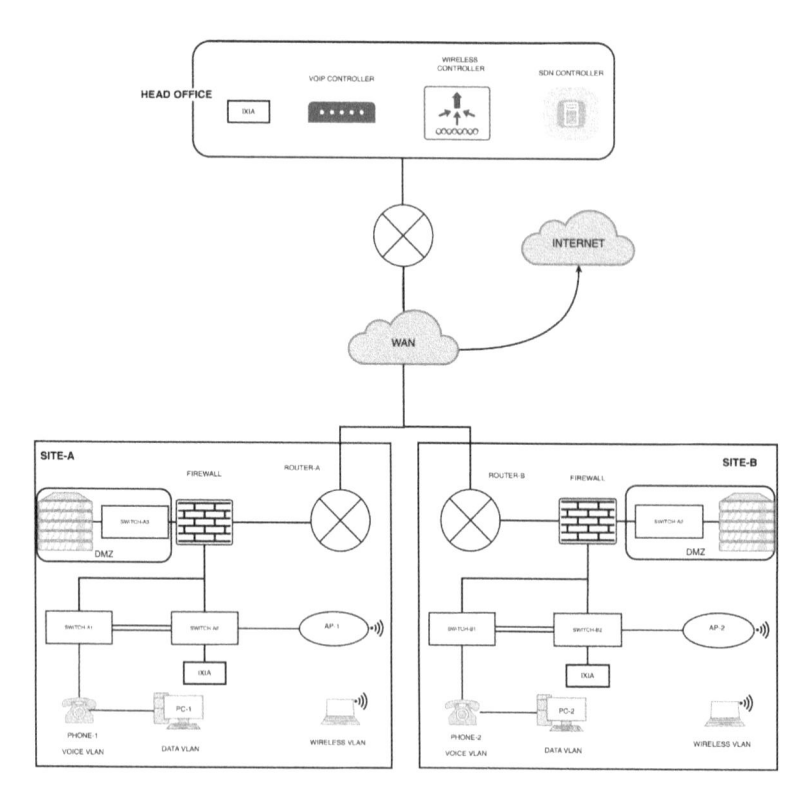

Fig-9.1.1: Device and Platform Compatibility

Network Topology: A test network comprising routers, switches, and other network devices connected in various configurations.

Test Tools: Network management software, traffic generators, device emulation tools, virtualization platforms.

Test Cases:

I. **Hardware Compatibility Testing:**

   Test Scenario: Verify the compatibility of network devices with different hardware configurations, interfaces, and form factors.

   Test Steps:

   1. Connect network devices to various hardware components, such as servers, workstations, and network appliances.
   2. Test the functionality and performance of network devices in different hardware environments and configurations.

   Expected Result: Ensure that network devices can operate reliably and effectively with a wide range of hardware components and configurations without compatibility issues.

II. **Software Compatibility Testing:**

   Test Scenario: Validate the compatibility of network devices with different software versions, firmware releases, and operating systems.

   Test Steps:

   1. Install and configure network devices with different software versions, firmware updates, and patches.
   2. Test the functionality and performance of network devices with various software configurations and operating systems.

   Expected Result: Verify that network devices can seamlessly integrate with different software environments and operate without compatibility issues or conflicts.

III. **Protocol Compatibility Testing:**

   Test Scenario: Ensure that network devices support industry-standard protocols and are compatible with communication protocols used in diverse network environments.

   Test Steps:

   1. Configure network devices to communicate using different network protocols, such as TCP/IP, UDP, SNMP, and DHCP.
   2. Test interoperability and compatibility with devices from different vendors and platforms using common communication protocols.

Expected Result: Confirm that network devices can communicate effectively with other devices and platforms using standard networking protocols without protocol-related issues or incompatibilities.

IV. Interoperability Testing:

Test Scenario: Evaluate the interoperability of routers and switches with third-party devices, systems, and software solutions.

Test Steps:

1. Integrate network devices with third-party hardware, software applications, and network management systems.
2. Test the interaction and compatibility of network devices with third-party components in real-world network scenarios.

Expected Result: Ensure seamless interoperability and integration of network devices with third-party solutions without compatibility issues or performance degradation.

V. Vendor-specific Feature Testing:

Test Scenario: Validate the compatibility of network devices with vendor-specific features, proprietary protocols, and advanced functionalities.

Test Steps:

1. Configure network devices to utilize vendor-specific features and advanced functionalities, such as VLANs, QoS, and MPLS.
2. Test the functionality and performance of vendor-specific features in different network configurations and scenarios.

Expected Result: Verify that network devices can effectively leverage vendor-specific features and functionalities without compatibility issues or limitations.

Conclusion:

Compatibility testing for network devices plays a crucial role in ensuring seamless integration, interoperability, and performance across diverse network environments. By validating hardware compatibility, software compatibility, protocol compatibility, interoperability with third-party solutions, and vendor-specific feature compatibility, organizations can mitigate compatibility issues, enhance network reliability, and optimize the performance of their network infrastructure. Effective compatibility testing helps ensure that network devices can operate seamlessly with different hardware, software, and platforms, facilitating the deployment of robust and scalable network solutions in complex network environments.

9.2. Interoperability Testing

Interoperability testing ensures that network devices from different vendors can communicate and work together effectively within a network environment. This testing verifies that devices adhere to industry standards and protocols, enabling seamless integration and interoperability across heterogeneous network infrastructures. Let's explore an example of interoperability testing for network devices, focusing on routers and switches from different vendors.

Example: Interoperability Testing for Network Devices

Objective: Validate the interoperability of routers and switches from different vendors to ensure seamless communication and integration in a multi-vendor network environment.

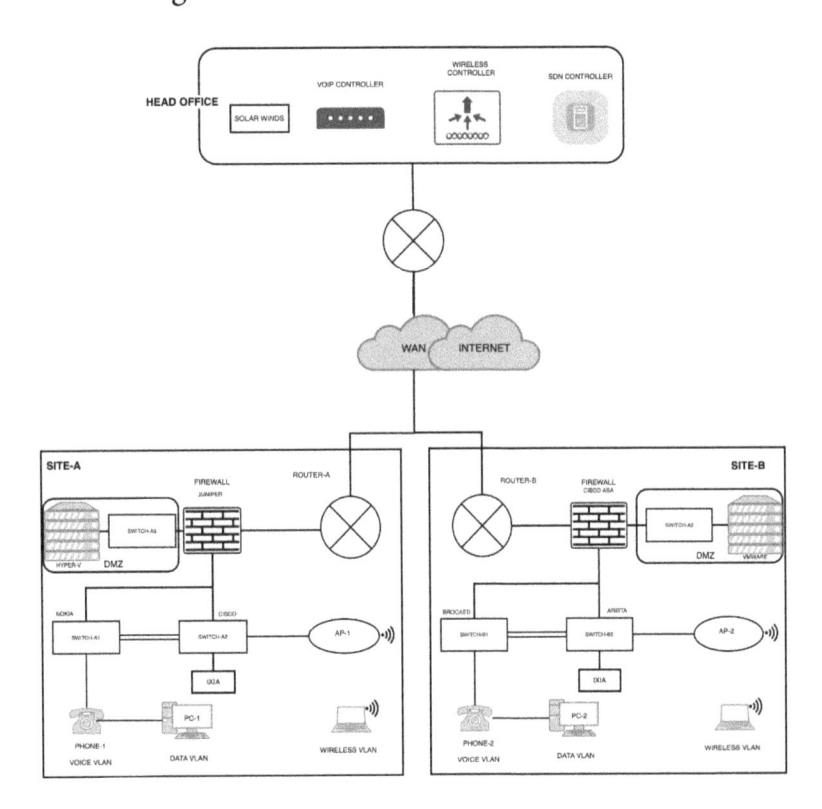

Fig-9.2.1: Interoperability Testing for Network Devices

Test Setup:

Network Topology: A test network comprising routers and switches from different vendors interconnected in various configurations.

Test Tools: Network management software, protocol analyzers, traffic generators, device emulation tools.

Test Cases:

I. **Basic Connectivity Testing:**

Test Scenario: Verify basic connectivity and communication between routers and switches from different vendors.

Test Steps:

1. Connect routers and switches from different vendors in various network topologies, such as point-to-point, star, and mesh networks.

2. Test the ability of devices to exchange routing information, forward traffic, and establish Layer 2 and Layer 3 connections.

Expected Result: Ensure that routers and switches can communicate and interoperate effectively regardless of vendor-specific implementations or protocols.

II. VLAN Configuration and Trunking:

Test Scenario: Validate the interoperability of VLAN configurations and trunking protocols (e.g., IEEE 802.1Q) between devices from different vendors.

Test Steps:

1. Configure VLANs and trunking interfaces on routers and switches from different vendors.
2. Test the ability to propagate VLAN information, establish trunk links, and forward VLAN-tagged traffic between devices.

Expected Result: Verify that VLAN configurations and trunking protocols are interoperable and function correctly across heterogeneous network devices.

III. Dynamic Routing Protocol Compatibility:

Test Scenario: Evaluate the interoperability of dynamic routing protocols (e.g., OSPF, EIGRP, BGP) between routers from different vendors.

Test Steps:

1. Configure routers to run dynamic routing protocols and exchange routing information with routers from different vendors.
2. Monitor routing updates, route advertisements, and routing table synchronization to ensure seamless interoperability.

Expected Result: Confirm that routers can exchange routing information and dynamically adapt to changes in network topology without protocol-related issues.

IV. Quality of Service (QoS) Interoperability:

Test Scenario: Validate the interoperability of QoS features and policies across switches and routers from different vendors.

Test Steps:

1. Configure QoS parameters, such as traffic classification, prioritization, and queuing mechanisms, on network devices.
2. Test the ability to apply QoS policies consistently and enforce traffic prioritization and bandwidth management across heterogeneous devices.

Expected Result: Ensure that QoS features and policies are interoperable and effectively applied to prioritize critical traffic and optimize network performance.

V. Security Protocol Interoperability:

Test Scenario: Assess the interoperability of security protocols and mechanisms (e.g., IPsec, SSL/TLS) between routers and switches from different vendors.

Test Steps:

1. Configure security protocols and encryption settings on network devices to establish secure communication channels.
2. Test the ability to negotiate security parameters, authenticate peers, and encrypt traffic across heterogeneous devices.

Expected Result: Verify that security protocols and mechanisms are interoperable and provide secure communication between devices from different vendors.

Conclusion:

Interoperability testing for network devices is essential for ensuring seamless communication and integration in multi-vendor network environments. By validating basic connectivity, VLAN configuration, dynamic routing protocol compatibility, QoS interoperability, and security protocol compatibility, organizations can mitigate interoperability issues, enhance network reliability, and optimize the performance of their network infrastructure. Effective interoperability testing facilitates the deployment of heterogeneous network solutions, enabling organizations to leverage best-of-breed technologies and vendor offerings to meet their specific networking requirements.

9.3. Browser Compatibility

Browser compatibility testing ensures that network management interfaces, configuration portals, and web-based applications hosted on network devices are accessible and function correctly across different web browsers and versions. This testing verifies that users can effectively interact with network devices using their preferred web browsers without encountering compatibility issues or functionality limitations. Let's explore an example of browser compatibility testing for network devices, focusing on the management interface of a router.

Example: Browser Compatibility Testing for Router Management Interface

Objective: Validate the compatibility of a router's management interface with various web browsers to ensure accessibility and functionality across different browser environments.

Test Setup:

Router Model: XYZ Router

Management Interface: Web-based configuration portal accessed via a web browser

Test Tools: Multiple web browsers (e.g., Google Chrome, Mozilla Firefox, Microsoft Edge), browser testing tools (e.g., BrowserStack, Sauce Labs), network traffic monitoring tools.

Test Cases:

I. Cross-browser Functionality Testing:

Test Scenario: Verify the functionality of the router's management interface across different web browsers and versions.

Test Steps:

1. Access the router's management interface using various web browsers, including Google Chrome, Mozilla Firefox, Microsoft Edge, Safari, and Opera.
2. Perform common management tasks, such as configuration changes, firmware updates, and status monitoring, in each browser.

Expected Result: Ensure that all essential functions of the router's management interface are accessible and perform correctly across different web browsers without errors or inconsistencies.

II. User Interface Rendering Testing:

Test Scenario: Evaluate the consistency and accuracy of the router's user interface rendering across different web browsers and screen resolutions.

Test Steps:

1. View the router's management interface in various web browsers with different screen sizes and resolutions, including desktop and mobile devices.
2. Verify that UI elements, layout, styling, and graphical components render consistently and correctly in each browser environment.

Expected Result: Confirm that the router's management interface displays uniformly across different web browsers and devices, maintaining usability and accessibility for users.

III. Browser-specific Compatibility Testing:

Test Scenario: Identify and address browser-specific compatibility issues or limitations that may affect the functionality or user experience of the router's management interface.

Test Steps:

1. Test the router's management interface in each supported web browser for compatibility issues, such as JavaScript errors, CSS rendering issues, or browser-specific behaviors.
2. Document any observed discrepancies or inconsistencies in functionality, layout, or performance between browsers.

Expected Result: Address browser-specific compatibility issues through remediation efforts, such as code adjustments, feature detection, or browser-specific workarounds, to ensure uniform functionality and user experience across all supported browsers.

IV. Performance Testing:

Test Scenario: Assess the performance and responsiveness of the router's management interface under different browser environments and network conditions.

Test Steps:

1. Access the router's management interface using various web browsers on devices with different hardware specifications and network connections.
2. Measure and compare the load times, response times, and overall performance metrics of the interface in each browser environment.

Expected Result: Ensure that the router's management interface delivers consistent performance and responsiveness across different browsers and devices, maintaining usability and efficiency for users.

Conclusion:

Browser compatibility testing for network devices' management interfaces is essential for ensuring accessibility, functionality, and user experience consistency across diverse web browser environments. By validating cross-browser functionality, UI rendering, browser-specific compatibility, and performance characteristics, organizations can mitigate compatibility issues, enhance user satisfaction, and optimize the usability of their network management interfaces. Effective browser compatibility testing facilitates seamless interaction with network devices, empowering users to configure, monitor, and manage their network infrastructure effectively across various web browsers and platforms.

In addition to device and platform compatibility, interoperability testing, and browser compatibility, there are several other areas that can be covered in compatibility testing for network devices. Here are a few additional aspects to consider:

V. Operating System Compatibility:

- Verify that network device management software, drivers, and utilities are compatible with different operating systems (e.g., Windows, macOS, Linux).
- Test installation, configuration, and functionality across various operating system versions and distributions.

VI. Mobile Compatibility:

- Assess the compatibility of network device management interfaces with mobile devices (e.g., smartphones, tablets).
- Test responsiveness, usability, and functionality of web-based interfaces on mobile browsers and mobile operating systems (e.g., iOS, Android).

VII. Database Compatibility:

- Validate compatibility with different database management systems (DBMS) used for storing configuration data, logs, and performance metrics.
- Test integration, data exchange, and performance with commonly used databases (e.g., MySQL, PostgreSQL, Microsoft SQL Server).

VIII. Localization and Internationalization Compatibility:

- Ensure that network device management interfaces support localization (translation into multiple languages) and internationalization (support for various cultural conventions).
- Test language support, character encoding, date/time formats, and currency symbols to accommodate users from different regions and languages.

IX. Accessibility Compatibility:

- Verify compliance with accessibility standards (e.g., WCAG) to ensure that network device management interfaces are accessible to users with disabilities.
- Test compatibility with assistive technologies (e.g., screen readers, keyboard navigation) and adherence to accessibility guidelines for usability and inclusivity.

X. Firmware and Software Version Compatibility:

- Validate compatibility between network devices and firmware/software versions to ensure smooth upgrades and compatibility with new features.
- Test backward compatibility with older firmware/software versions and forward compatibility with future releases.

XI. Third-party Integration Compatibility:

- Assess compatibility with third-party software, applications, and tools commonly used in network management and administration (e.g., network monitoring systems, configuration management platforms).
- Test interoperability, data exchange, and integration capabilities to ensure seamless integration with external systems and workflows.

XII. API Compatibility:

- Validate compatibility and adherence to API specifications for network device management interfaces.
- Test functionality, data exchange, and security of APIs used for automation, integration, and external system interaction.

XIII. Hardware Compatibility:

- Verify compatibility with third-party hardware components and peripherals commonly used in conjunction with network devices (e.g., network interface cards, expansion modules).
- Test functionality, performance, and interoperability with compatible hardware configurations.

By covering these additional areas in compatibility testing, organizations can ensure that network devices seamlessly integrate with diverse environments, platforms, and user requirements, maximizing usability, performance, and user satisfaction. Effective compatibility testing helps mitigate compatibility issues, enhance interoperability, and optimize the functionality and usability of network devices across various usage scenarios and environments.

CHAPTER 10

STRESS TESTING

10.1. Overload and Stability Testing

Stress testing evaluates the performance and stability of network devices under extreme conditions, such as high traffic loads, resource exhaustion, and adverse network conditions. Overload and stability testing specifically focus on assessing how network devices handle heavy workloads and maintain operational stability under stress. Let's delve into an example of overload and stability testing for network devices, using routers as the primary example.

Example: Overload and Stability Testing for Routers

Objective: Assess the performance, scalability, and stability of routers under high traffic loads and adverse network conditions to identify potential bottlenecks and stability issues.

Test Setup:

Router Model: XYZ Router

Network Topology: A simulated network environment with multiple routers interconnected in various configurations.

Traffic Generation Tools: Network traffic generators (e.g., Iperf, D-ITG) to simulate high traffic loads and network congestion.

Monitoring Tools: Network monitoring software (e.g., SNMP monitoring tools, Wireshark) to track router performance metrics and network traffic.

Test Cases:

I. **Maximum Throughput Testing:**

Test Scenario: Determine the maximum throughput capacity of the router by subjecting it to gradually increasing traffic loads.

Test Steps:

1. Configure the router and network environment to handle the maximum expected traffic load.
2. Gradually increase the traffic load generated by traffic generators until the router reaches its maximum throughput capacity.
3. Monitor router performance metrics, such as packet loss, latency, and throughput, to identify performance degradation or stability issues.

Expected Result: Determine the maximum throughput capacity of the router and identify any performance limitations or bottlenecks under heavy traffic loads.

II. Long-duration Stress Testing:

Test Scenario: Evaluate the router's stability and resilience by subjecting it to sustained high traffic loads over an extended period.

Test Steps:

1. Continuously generate high volumes of network traffic using traffic generators to stress the router.
2. Monitor router performance metrics and network behavior over an extended duration (e.g., several hours or days).
3. Analyze router logs, error messages, and performance data to assess stability and identify any signs of degradation or failure.

Expected Result: Confirm that the router maintains stable operation and sustains performance under prolonged stress conditions without crashes, freezes, or significant performance degradation.

III. Concurrent Connections Testing:

Test Scenario: Evaluate the router's ability to handle a large number of concurrent connections and sessions.

Test Steps:

1. Establish a large number of concurrent connections to the router, simulating real-world usage scenarios.
2. Monitor router resource utilization, CPU/memory usage, and session establishment/teardown rates.
3. Increase the number of concurrent connections until the router reaches its maximum supported capacity or exhibits performance degradation.

Expected Result: Determine the maximum number of concurrent connections the router can handle while maintaining stable operation and acceptable performance levels.

IV. Denial-of-Service (DoS) Attack Simulation:

Test Scenario: Assess the router's resilience against DoS attacks by simulating various attack scenarios.

Test Steps:

1. Simulate DoS attack scenarios, such as SYN flood, ICMP flood, or UDP flood attacks, targeting the router.
2. Monitor router behavior, performance metrics, and response times during the attack simulation.
3. Evaluate the router's ability to detect, mitigate, and recover from DoS attacks without service disruption or performance degradation.

Expected Result: Confirm that the router implements effective DoS attack mitigation measures and maintains operational stability during attack simulations.

Conclusion:

Overload and stability testing for routers is crucial for assessing their performance, scalability, and resilience under heavy traffic loads and adverse network conditions. By conducting maximum throughput testing, long-duration stress testing, concurrent connections testing, and DoS attack simulations, organizations can identify performance limitations, stability issues, and potential vulnerabilities in router deployments. Effective stress testing helps ensure that routers can handle high traffic loads, maintain stable operation, and deliver reliable performance in real-world network environments, enhancing network reliability and resilience.

10.2. Resource Exhaustion Testing

Resource exhaustion testing assesses the ability of network devices to handle sustained high workloads without depleting critical system resources, such as CPU, memory, and storage. This type of stress testing helps identify potential resource bottlenecks and stability issues that may arise under heavy operational loads. Let's explore an example of resource exhaustion testing for network devices, focusing on switches.

Example: Resource Exhaustion Testing for Switches

Objective: Evaluate the performance and stability of switches under prolonged high traffic loads to identify resource exhaustion issues and potential bottlenecks.

Test Setup:

Switch Model: XYZ Switch

Network Topology: A simulated network environment with multiple switches interconnected in various configurations.

Traffic Generation Tools: Network traffic generators (e.g., Iperf, D-ITG) to simulate high traffic loads and network congestion.

Monitoring Tools: Network monitoring software (e.g., SNMP monitoring tools, CLI commands) to track switch performance metrics and resource utilization.

Test Cases:

I. **CPU Utilization Testing:**

   Test Scenario: Assess the switch's CPU utilization under sustained high traffic loads to identify potential CPU bottlenecks.

   Test Steps:

   1. Generate continuous traffic flows through the switch using traffic generators to stress the device's forwarding capabilities.

2. Monitor the switch's CPU utilization using SNMP monitoring tools or CLI commands.

3. Increase the traffic load incrementally and observe CPU utilization trends to identify thresholds where CPU resources become saturated.

Expected Result: Determine the maximum sustainable traffic load that the switch can handle without experiencing excessive CPU utilization and performance degradation.

II. Memory Consumption Testing:

Test Scenario: Evaluate the switch's memory usage and stability under prolonged high traffic loads to detect potential memory leaks or exhaustion.

Test Steps:

1. Continuously generate traffic through the switch to induce memory-intensive operations, such as packet buffering and table management.

2. Monitor the switch's memory usage, including buffer utilization, packet memory allocation, and table sizes.

3. Analyze memory usage patterns over time to identify any abnormal increases or memory exhaustion points.

Expected Result: Ensure that the switch maintains stable memory usage levels and does not experience memory exhaustion or leaks under sustained traffic loads.

III. Forwarding Performance Testing:

Test Scenario: Measure the switch's forwarding performance and packet processing capabilities under heavy traffic loads to assess throughput and latency.

Test Steps:

1. Configure the switch to forward traffic between multiple network segments or VLANs.

2. Generate traffic flows at maximum line rate through the switch and measure throughput and latency metrics.

3. Increase traffic loads gradually and observe any degradation in forwarding performance or increases in packet latency.

Expected Result: Validate that the switch maintains consistent forwarding performance and low latency under increasing traffic loads without dropping packets or introducing significant delays.

IV. Buffer Management Testing:

Test Scenario: Evaluate the switch's buffer management mechanisms and buffer overflow handling under sustained traffic loads.

Test Steps:

1. Generate traffic bursts or congestion scenarios to fill switch buffers and induce buffer overflow conditions.

2. Monitor buffer utilization and buffer overflow events to assess the switch's ability to manage buffer resources effectively.

3. Measure packet loss rates and observe switch behavior during buffer overflow conditions.

Expected Result: Confirm that the switch implements effective buffer management strategies to mitigate packet loss and maintain stable operation under congested network conditions.

Conclusion:

Resource exhaustion testing for switches is essential for identifying potential performance bottlenecks, stability issues, and resource limitations under sustained high traffic loads. By assessing CPU utilization, memory consumption, forwarding performance, and buffer management capabilities, organizations can ensure that switches can handle heavy workloads without experiencing resource depletion or degradation in performance. Effective resource exhaustion testing helps optimize network reliability, performance, and scalability by identifying and addressing potential resource constraints in switch deployments.

10.3. Failover and Recovery Testing

Failover and recovery testing assesses the ability of network devices to maintain operational continuity and recover from failures or disruptions effectively. This type of stress testing evaluates the resilience and fault tolerance mechanisms implemented in network devices to ensure uninterrupted service delivery in the event of failures or adverse conditions. Let's explore an example of failover and recovery testing for network devices, focusing on routers.

Example: Failover and Recovery Testing for Routers

Objective: Evaluate the failover and recovery capabilities of routers to ensure seamless operation and minimal downtime in the event of failures or disruptions.

Test Setup:

Router Model: XYZ Router

Network Topology: A redundant network topology with multiple routers configured for failover and redundancy.

Traffic Generation Tools: Network traffic generators (e.g., Iperf, D-ITG) to simulate traffic loads and disruptions.

Monitoring Tools: Network monitoring software (e.g., SNMP monitoring tools, syslog servers) to track router status and performance metrics.

Test Cases:

I. **Route Failover Testing:**

Test Scenario: Simulate a failure scenario by causing a primary router to become unavailable and verify that traffic is rerouted through a backup or secondary router.

Test Steps:

1. Configure router redundancy protocols such as VRRP (Virtual Router Redundancy Protocol) or HSRP (Hot Standby Router Protocol) to establish failover capabilities.

2. Generate traffic through the network and monitor routing tables and traffic paths to ensure that traffic is rerouted to the backup router upon primary router failure.

3. Validate the time taken for the failover process and assess any impact on network performance or service availability.

Expected Result: Confirm that failover occurs seamlessly and transparently to end-users, with minimal disruption to network services.

II. **Link Failover Testing:**

Test Scenario: Simulate link failures or network outages and verify that routers detect and respond to the failures by rerouting traffic through alternative paths.

Test Steps:

1. Introduce network disruptions such as link failures, interface flapping, or network congestion to trigger failover events.

2. Monitor router interfaces, link status, and routing updates to verify that routers detect the failures and adjust routing accordingly.

3. Validate the convergence time for link failover and assess any impact on network performance or packet loss.

Expected Result: Ensure that routers quickly detect and respond to link failures, rerouting traffic through alternative paths to maintain connectivity and service availability.

III. **Configuration Recovery Testing:**

Test Scenario: Evaluate the router's ability to recover from configuration changes, firmware upgrades, or software updates without service interruption.

Test Steps:

1. Perform configuration changes or software upgrades on the router, such as modifying routing policies, updating access control lists (ACLs), or installing firmware updates.

2. Monitor router behavior during the configuration changes or upgrades to assess any impact on network services or performance.

3. Verify that the router reverts to its previous state or applies the new configuration without disrupting ongoing network operations.

Expected Result: Confirm that the router can recover from configuration changes or upgrades seamlessly, maintaining service continuity and adhering to defined network policies.

IV. High Availability Testing:

Test Scenario: Assess the overall high availability of the router deployment by simulating various failure scenarios and verifying failover mechanisms.

Test Steps:

1. Create a comprehensive test plan covering different failure scenarios, including hardware failures, software crashes, and network partitioning events.
2. Execute the test plan to simulate failure scenarios and monitor router behavior, failover events, and service availability.
3. Analyze test results to identify any weaknesses or areas for improvement in the router's high availability mechanisms.

Expected Result: Ensure that the router deployment exhibits robust high availability characteristics, with failover mechanisms effectively mitigating failures and ensuring uninterrupted service delivery.

Conclusion:

Failover and recovery testing for routers is crucial for ensuring continuous operation and minimal downtime in network deployments. By evaluating route failover, link failover, configuration recovery, and overall high availability capabilities, organizations can identify potential weaknesses and enhance the resilience of their router deployments. Effective failover and recovery testing help optimize network reliability, minimize service disruptions, and maintain seamless connectivity in the face of failures or disruptions.

In addition to overload and stability testing, resource exhaustion testing, and failover and recovery testing, there are several other areas that can be covered in stress testing for network devices. Here are a few additional aspects to consider:

V. Resilience to Network Attacks:

- Evaluate the network device's resilience to various types of network attacks, such as Distributed Denial of Service (DDoS) attacks, spoofing attacks, and protocol-based attacks.
- Test the device's ability to detect, mitigate, and recover from attacks without service interruption or performance degradation.

VI. Redundancy and High Availability Testing:

- Assess the redundancy and high availability mechanisms implemented in the network device, such as hardware redundancy, protocol-based redundancy, and geographic redundancy.
- Test failover mechanisms, redundancy protocols, and recovery procedures to ensure uninterrupted service delivery in the event of component failures or network disruptions.

VII. Load Balancing and Traffic Distribution Testing:

- Evaluate the network device's ability to distribute traffic evenly across multiple paths or resources to optimize performance and avoid congestion.

➢ Test load balancing algorithms, traffic distribution policies, and failover mechanisms to ensure efficient utilization of network resources under varying load conditions.

VIII. Resilience to Firmware/Software Bugs:

➢ Assess the network device's resilience to firmware or software bugs, glitches, or vulnerabilities that may impact performance, stability, or security.

➢ Test firmware/software upgrades, patches, and updates to verify their compatibility, reliability, and effectiveness in addressing known issues or vulnerabilities.

IX. Recovery from Environmental Factors:

➢ Evaluate the network device's ability to recover from environmental factors such as power outages, temperature fluctuations, and physical damage.

➢ Test power redundancy mechanisms, environmental monitoring systems, and physical security measures to ensure device resilience in challenging operating conditions.

X. Scale Testing:

➢ Assess the scalability of the network device to handle increasing workloads, network growth, and expansion requirements.

➢ Test the device's performance, throughput, and resource utilization under scaled-up configurations to identify scalability limits and potential bottlenecks.

XI. Resilience to Configuration Errors:

➢ Evaluate the network device's ability to recover from misconfigurations, human errors, or configuration conflicts that may impact performance or stability.

➢ Test configuration rollback mechanisms, error recovery procedures, and automated validation tools to ensure device resilience in the face of configuration-related issues.

XII. Disaster Recovery Testing:

➢ Assess the network device's readiness to recover from catastrophic events or disasters that may cause widespread infrastructure failures or data loss.

➢ Test disaster recovery plans, backup and recovery procedures, and data replication mechanisms to ensure business continuity and data integrity in worst-case scenarios.

By covering these additional areas in stress testing for network devices, organizations can identify and mitigate potential weaknesses, enhance device resilience, and optimize network reliability and performance in challenging operating conditions. Effective stress testing helps ensure that network devices can withstand the demands of real-world environments and deliver consistent, reliable performance under varying load conditions and unforeseen challenges.

CHAPTER 11
REPORTING AND DOCUMENTATION

11.1. Importance of Comprehensive Reporting

Comprehensive reporting and documentation are essential aspects of network device testing, providing valuable insights, analysis, and documentation of testing activities, results, and findings. Through detailed reporting, stakeholders can gain visibility into the testing process, understand the outcomes, and make informed decisions to address identified issues and improve network device performance and reliability. Let's explore the importance of comprehensive reporting using an example of testing a networking device topology.

Example: Comprehensive Reporting for Networking Device Testing Topology

Objective: Demonstrate the importance of comprehensive reporting in testing a networking device topology, focusing on identifying and addressing performance issues and optimizing network device configuration.

Test Setup:

Networking Device Topology: A complex network topology consisting of routers, switches, firewalls, and other network devices interconnected in various configurations.

Testing Tools: Network testing tools (e.g., traffic generators, monitoring software), configuration management tools, documentation tools.

Test Scenarios: Various testing scenarios covering functional testing, performance testing, security testing, and interoperability testing.

Key Components of Comprehensive Reporting:

1. Test Plan and Objectives:
   - Document the test plan outlining the objectives, scope, and methodologies of the testing activities.
   - Define testing scenarios, test cases, success criteria, and expected outcomes for each testing phase.
2. Testing Procedures and Execution:
   - Detail the testing procedures followed, including test environment setup, configuration parameters, and testing methodologies.

- Document the execution of test cases, including any deviations from the planned test scenarios and unexpected observations.

3. Test Results and Findings:
- Present detailed test results, performance metrics, and observations gathered during testing.
- Highlight any anomalies, failures, or performance bottlenecks identified during testing, along with their impact on network device functionality and performance.

4. Analysis and Recommendations:
- Analyze the test results to identify root causes of issues, performance limitations, or configuration errors.
- Provide recommendations and corrective actions to address identified issues, optimize network device configuration, and improve performance and reliability.

5. Risk Assessment and Mitigation:
- Assess the risks associated with identified issues, performance limitations, or configuration vulnerabilities.
- Propose risk mitigation strategies, including prioritization of issues, implementation of workarounds, and adoption of preventive measures.

6. Documentation of Configuration Changes:
- Document any configuration changes made during testing, including before-and-after snapshots of device configurations.
- Ensure that configuration changes are well-documented, tracked, and validated to maintain configuration integrity and compliance.

7. Lessons Learned and Best Practices:
- Capture lessons learned from the testing process, including insights, challenges encountered, and successful strategies employed.
- Share best practices, tips, and recommendations for future testing efforts and network device deployments.

Benefits of Comprehensive Reporting:
1. Transparency and Accountability:
- Provides stakeholders with transparency into the testing process, results, and findings, fostering accountability and trust in testing outcomes.

2. Decision Support:
- Empowers decision-makers with actionable insights and recommendations to address identified issues, prioritize improvements, and optimize network device performance.

3. Continuous Improvement:
   - Facilitates continuous improvement by documenting lessons learned, best practices, and recommendations for future testing efforts and network device deployments.

4. Risk Management:
   - Enables effective risk management by identifying and addressing performance limitations, configuration errors, and security vulnerabilities in network device deployments.

5. Compliance and Auditability:
   - Supports compliance requirements by documenting testing procedures, results, and corrective actions taken to ensure adherence to industry standards and regulatory mandates.

Conclusion:

Comprehensive reporting and documentation play a crucial role in network device testing, providing stakeholders with visibility, insights, and actionable recommendations to optimize device performance, reliability, and security. By documenting testing procedures, results, findings, and recommendations in a structured and comprehensive manner, organizations can improve decision-making, mitigate risks, and drive continuous improvement in network device deployments. Effective reporting enables stakeholders to make informed decisions, address identified issues, and enhance the overall performance and resilience of network infrastructure.

11.2. Documenting Test Results

Documenting test results is a critical aspect of network device testing, providing a detailed record of testing activities, outcomes, and findings. Comprehensive documentation ensures transparency, accountability, and traceability of testing efforts, facilitating effective analysis, decision-making, and improvement of network device performance and reliability. Let's explore the importance of documenting test results using an example of testing a networking device topology.

Example: Documenting Test Results for Networking Device Testing Topology

Objective: Illustrate the importance of documenting test results in testing a networking device topology, focusing on capturing detailed information about testing activities, outcomes, and findings.

Test Setup:

Networking Device Topology: A complex network topology comprising routers, switches, firewalls, and other network devices interconnected in various configurations.

Testing Tools: Network testing tools (e.g., traffic generators, monitoring software), configuration management tools, documentation tools.

Test Scenarios: Various testing scenarios covering functional testing, performance testing, security testing, and interoperability testing.

Key Components of Documenting Test Results:

1. Test Summary:
   - Provide an overview of the testing objectives, scope, and methodologies employed.
   - Summarize the key findings, observations, and conclusions derived from testing activities.
2. Test Environment Configuration:
   - Document the configuration details of the test environment, including hardware specifications, software versions, and network topology diagrams.
   - Capture any variations or changes made to the test environment throughout the testing process.
3. Test Execution Logs:
   - Record detailed logs of test execution activities, including test cases executed, test outcomes, and any errors or issues encountered.
   - Document timestamps, test parameters, and relevant metrics collected during test execution.
4. Test Results Analysis:
   - Present a comprehensive analysis of test results, including performance metrics, security vulnerabilities, and interoperability issues identified.
   - Provide insights into the root causes of identified issues, potential impact on network device functionality, and recommended corrective actions.
5. Graphical Representations:
   - Include graphical representations of test results, such as charts, graphs, and diagrams, to visually depict performance trends, network traffic patterns, and security vulnerabilities.
   - Use visual aids to enhance understanding and interpretation of complex test data and findings.
6. Detailed Observations and Findings:
   - Document detailed observations and findings from testing activities, including strengths, weaknesses, and areas for improvement in network device performance and functionality.
   - Highlight any deviations from expected behavior, anomalies, or unexpected behaviors observed during testing.
7. Screenshots and Captures:
   - Include screenshots, captures, or recordings of critical test scenarios, network configurations, and error messages encountered during testing.
   - Provide visual evidence to support test findings, facilitate troubleshooting, and aid in the reproduction of identified issues.
8. Recommendations and Action Items:
   - Propose recommendations and action items based on test results and findings to address identified issues, optimize network device configuration, and enhance overall performance and reliability.

➤ Prioritize recommendations based on severity, impact, and urgency to guide decision-making and implementation efforts.

Benefits of Documenting Test Results:

1. Traceability and Accountability:
   ➤ Establish a clear trail of testing activities, outcomes, and findings to ensure accountability and traceability throughout the testing process.

2. Decision Support:
   ➤ Provide stakeholders with actionable insights and recommendations derived from test results to support informed decision-making and problem resolution.

3. Continuous Improvement:
   ➤ Facilitate continuous improvement by capturing lessons learned, best practices, and areas for enhancement identified during testing activities.

4. Knowledge Preservation:
   ➤ Preserve institutional knowledge and expertise by documenting test results, methodologies, and insights for future reference and training purposes.

5. Auditing and Compliance:
   ➤ Support auditing and compliance requirements by maintaining comprehensive records of testing activities, results, and corrective actions taken to ensure adherence to industry standards and regulatory mandates.

Conclusion:

Documenting test results is essential for ensuring transparency, accountability, and traceability in network device testing. By capturing detailed information about testing activities, outcomes, and findings, organizations can analyze test data effectively, make informed decisions, and drive continuous improvement in network device performance and reliability. Comprehensive documentation facilitates collaboration, knowledge sharing, and problem-solving efforts, ultimately enhancing the effectiveness and efficiency of network device testing initiatives.

11.3. Communicating Findings to Stakeholders

Effectively communicating testing results and findings to stakeholders is crucial for ensuring transparency, understanding, and actionable insights. Stakeholders, including project sponsors, management teams, and technical personnel, rely on clear and concise reporting to make informed decisions and prioritize actions. Let's explore the importance of communicating testing results to stakeholders in the context of networking devices testing, along with best practices, templates, and recommendations.

Importance of Communicating Testing Results to Stakeholders:

1. Alignment of Objectives:
   - Communicating testing results ensures that stakeholders are aligned with the objectives, scope, and outcomes of the testing activities. Clear communication helps establish common goals and expectations among project participants.

2. Informed Decision-Making:
   - Stakeholders require accurate and timely information to make informed decisions regarding network device configurations, optimizations, and investments. Communicating testing results provides stakeholders with the data needed to prioritize actions and allocate resources effectively.

3. Risk Awareness and Mitigation:
   - Testing results highlight potential risks, vulnerabilities, and issues identified during testing, enabling stakeholders to proactively mitigate risks and address critical issues before they escalate into significant problems or security breaches.

4. Continuous Improvement:
   - Transparent communication of testing results fosters a culture of continuous improvement by facilitating knowledge sharing, lessons learned, and best practices across project teams and organizational units. Stakeholders can leverage insights from testing results to refine processes, enhance configurations, and optimize network performance.

Communicating Testing Results to Stakeholders:

1. Tailor Reports to Audience Needs:
   - Customize reports to suit the specific needs and preferences of different stakeholder groups. Tailor the level of detail, technical complexity, and presentation format to ensure that reports are relevant and comprehensible to diverse audiences.

2. Provide Context and Analysis:
   - Contextualize testing results within the broader context of network infrastructure, business objectives, and industry standards. Offer analysis, insights, and interpretations to help stakeholders understand the implications of test findings and prioritize action items accordingly.

3. Use Visual Aids and Graphics:
   - Enhance the readability and comprehension of reports by incorporating visual aids, graphics, and charts to illustrate key findings, trends, and performance metrics. Visual representations can convey complex information more effectively than text alone.

4. Highlight Key Findings and Recommendations:

- Clearly identify and prioritize key findings, observations, and recommendations in the reporting. Use headings, bullet points, or call-out boxes to emphasize critical insights and action items for stakeholders' attention.

5. Provide Actionable Recommendations:
- Offer actionable recommendations for addressing identified issues, mitigating risks, and optimizing network device performance and security. Present recommendations in a clear, concise manner, accompanied by implementation guidelines and timelines.

6. Facilitate Two-Way Communication:
- Foster open dialogue and two-way communication channels to encourage stakeholder engagement and feedback on testing results. Solicit input, questions, and concerns from stakeholders to ensure that reporting meets their information needs and expectations.

Reporting Template **Example:**

[Sample Networking Devices Testing Results Report]

1. Executive Summary:
- Provides a high-level overview of key testing results, findings, and recommendations.

2. Introduction:
- Briefly outlines the objectives, scope, and methodologies of the testing activities.

3. Testing Environment:
- Describes the network topology, equipment configurations, and testing scenarios used during testing.

4. Summary of Testing Results:
- Presents summarized findings, observations, and performance metrics for each tested network device.

5. Detailed Test Results:
- Provides detailed test results, including performance metrics, error rates, and identified issues, for each tested network device.

6. Analysis and Interpretation:
- Offers analysis, insights, and interpretations of test findings, highlighting trends, patterns, and potential implications for stakeholders.

7. Recommendations for Action:
- Proposes actionable recommendations for addressing identified issues, mitigating risks, and optimizing network device performance and security.

8. **Conclusion:**
   - Summarizes key findings, conclusions, and next steps for stakeholders' consideration.
9. Appendices:
   - Includes supplementary information, detailed test data, and additional documentation for reference.

Recommendations:

1. Establish Regular Reporting Cadence:
   - Schedule regular reporting intervals aligned with project milestones and stakeholder expectations. Consistent reporting cadence ensures that stakeholders receive timely updates on testing progress and outcomes.
2. Seek Stakeholder Feedback and Engagement:
   - Encourage stakeholder engagement and participation throughout the reporting process. Solicit feedback, questions, and suggestions from stakeholders to ensure that reporting meets their information needs and fosters a collaborative approach to problem-solving.
3. Provide Opportunities for Clarification:
   - Offer opportunities for stakeholders to seek clarification or additional information on testing results as needed. Facilitate open dialogue and address stakeholders' questions or concerns promptly and comprehensively.

By adhering to best practices for communicating testing results to stakeholders, organizations can maximize the value of their testing efforts, drive informed decision-making, and foster collaboration and continuous improvement in network infrastructure management and performance optimization. Transparent communication builds trust, accountability, and shared understanding among project participants, ultimately leading to more effective and successful outcomes in network device testing initiatives.

Here are additional areas that can be covered in the "Reporting and Documentation" section:

4. Lessons Learned and Best Practices:
   - Reflect on lessons learned throughout the testing process, including challenges encountered, successes achieved, and areas for improvement. Document best practices and recommendations for future testing endeavors based on insights gained from the testing experience.
5. Documentation of Test Procedures and Methodologies:
   - Provide detailed documentation of the test procedures, methodologies, and configurations used during testing. This documentation ensures repeatability and transparency in the testing process and serves as a reference for future testing efforts.
6. Verification of Compliance and Standards:
   - Verify compliance with regulatory requirements, industry standards, and organizational policies related to network device testing. Document adherence to relevant standards and regulations, as well as any deviations or exceptions encountered during testing.

7. Impact Analysis and Change Management:
   - Conduct an impact analysis to assess the potential effects of testing findings on existing network configurations, policies, and operations. Document change management procedures for implementing recommended changes or remediation actions based on testing results.

8. Benchmarking and Performance Comparison:
   - Perform benchmarking and performance comparison analyses to evaluate the performance of network devices against industry benchmarks or competitor products. Document benchmarking results and performance comparisons to provide context for testing outcomes.

9. Historical Trend Analysis:
   - Analyze historical testing data and trends to identify patterns, anomalies, and areas of improvement over time. Document historical trend analysis findings to track performance trends, assess the effectiveness of remediation efforts, and guide future testing strategies.

10. Quality Assurance and Audit Trails:
    - Establish quality assurance processes and maintain audit trails to ensure the integrity and reliability of testing documentation. Document quality assurance activities, audit findings, and corrective actions taken to address identified deficiencies or discrepancies.

11. Documentation of Test Environments and Configurations:
    - Document the configurations and characteristics of test environments, including hardware, software, and network infrastructure components. Maintain up-to-date records of test environment configurations to facilitate reproducibility and troubleshooting.

12. User Documentation and Training Materials:
    - Develop user documentation and training materials based on testing findings and recommendations. Provide user guides, manuals, and training resources to educate stakeholders on optimal use and configuration of network devices.

13. Feedback and Continuous Improvement Mechanisms:
    - Establish mechanisms for collecting feedback from stakeholders on reporting and documentation practices. Use stakeholder feedback to identify areas for improvement and drive continuous enhancement of reporting and documentation processes.

14. Dissemination and Accessibility:
    - Ensure that reporting and documentation are easily accessible and disseminated to relevant stakeholders. Utilize appropriate channels and platforms for sharing reports, such as email distribution lists, project management tools, or document repositories.

By covering these additional areas in the "Reporting and Documentation" section, organizations can enhance the completeness, transparency, and effectiveness of their testing efforts. Comprehensive reporting and documentation practices support informed decision-making, facilitate compliance with standards and regulations, and drive continuous improvement in network device testing and management processes.

CHAPTER 12

REAL-WORLD CASE STUDIES

12.1. Success Stories

Real-world case studies provide valuable insights into the practical application and benefits of network device testing in diverse organizational contexts. Success stories highlight how organizations leverage testing methodologies, tools, and best practices to optimize network performance, enhance security, and mitigate risks. Let's explore a real-world case study showcasing a success story in network device testing.

Case Study: Optimizing Network Performance with Comprehensive Testing

Organization Background:

A global financial services company, XYZ Bank, operates a complex network infrastructure spanning multiple data centers, branches, and remote offices. The bank's network supports critical financial transactions, client communications, and internal operations, making performance, reliability, and security paramount.

Challenge:

XYZ Bank faced challenges in maintaining optimal network performance and reliability amidst increasing demands, evolving technologies, and growing security threats. The bank's network infrastructure, consisting of routers, switches, firewalls, and load balancers, required rigorous testing to identify bottlenecks, vulnerabilities, and areas for improvement.

Solution:

XYZ Bank engaged a team of network testing experts to conduct comprehensive testing of its network infrastructure, focusing on key performance indicators, security protocols, and high availability mechanisms. The testing methodology included functional testing, performance testing, security testing, and stress testing to assess the resilience, scalability, and reliability of network devices.

Testing Approach:

1. Functional Testing:
    - Verified the functionality and interoperability of network devices, ensuring seamless communication and data transfer across the network.

- Tested routing protocols, VLAN configurations, and Quality of Service (QoS) policies to validate network services and features.

2. Performance Testing:

- Evaluated bandwidth utilization, latency, and throughput across different network segments and traffic types.
- Conducted load testing and stress testing to assess the network's capacity to handle peak traffic loads and maintain performance under stress conditions.

3. Security Testing:

- Identified vulnerabilities, misconfigurations, and potential security loopholes in network devices.
- Conducted penetration testing, vulnerability scanning, and firewall rule analysis to enhance network security posture.

4. Stress Testing:

- Simulated real-world scenarios such as network congestion, hardware failures, and DDoS attacks to assess the resilience and fault tolerance of network devices.
- Tested failover mechanisms, redundancy protocols, and disaster recovery procedures to ensure business continuity in the event of failures or disruptions.

Results:

1. Optimized Network Performance:

- Network device testing revealed optimization opportunities, leading to the fine-tuning of configurations, routing policies, and traffic management strategies.
- Performance improvements, including reduced latency, increased bandwidth utilization, and enhanced throughput, resulted in a more responsive and efficient network infrastructure.

2. Enhanced Security Posture:

- Security testing identified and addressed vulnerabilities, ensuring compliance with industry regulations and protecting sensitive data assets.
- Implementation of enhanced security controls, including intrusion detection systems, access controls, and encryption protocols, strengthened the bank's security posture and mitigated cyber threats.

3. Improved Reliability and Resilience:

- Stress testing validated the resilience of network devices and failover mechanisms, minimizing downtime and service disruptions.
- High availability configurations, redundancy protocols, and disaster recovery procedures were optimized to ensure uninterrupted service delivery and business continuity.

Conclusion:

By leveraging comprehensive network device testing, XYZ Bank successfully optimized network performance, enhanced security, and improved reliability across its global infrastructure. Real-world case studies such as this demonstrate the tangible benefits of testing methodologies in mitigating risks, optimizing resource utilization, and ensuring the robustness of network infrastructures in demanding operational environments.

Key Takeaways:

- Comprehensive testing methodologies help organizations identify and address network performance bottlenecks, security vulnerabilities, and reliability concerns.
- Real-world case studies showcase the practical application and benefits of testing methodologies in optimizing network performance, enhancing security posture, and ensuring business continuity.
- By investing in network device testing, organizations can proactively identify and mitigate risks, optimize resource utilization, and enhance the overall resilience and reliability of their network infrastructures.

Real-world case studies serve as valuable examples of how organizations can leverage testing methodologies to overcome challenges, achieve business objectives, and drive continuous improvement in network performance and security.

12.2. Challenges Faced and Overcome

Real-world case studies offer insights into the challenges encountered during network device testing and the strategies employed to overcome them. These case studies provide valuable lessons learned and best practices for navigating complex testing scenarios and achieving successful outcomes. Let's explore a real-world case study highlighting challenges faced and overcome during network device testing.

Case Study: Overcoming Testing Challenges in a Large-scale Network Migration Project

Organization Background:

A multinational corporation, ABC Enterprises, embarked on a large-scale network migration project aimed at modernizing its infrastructure and enhancing operational efficiency. The project involved migrating legacy network devices to a new, state-of-the-art architecture, encompassing routers, switches, firewalls, and load balancers across multiple data centers and regional offices.

Challenges:

1. Legacy Infrastructure Compatibility:
   - Compatibility issues arose when integrating legacy network devices with modern technologies and protocols, leading to connectivity issues and interoperability challenges.

- Legacy devices lacked support for advanced features such as IPv6, multicast routing, and virtualization, complicating the migration process and requiring workaround solutions.

2. Complex Topology and Interdependencies:

- The network topology was highly complex, with interconnected devices, redundant paths, and intricate routing configurations spanning geographically dispersed locations.
- Mapping dependencies and understanding the impact of changes on interconnected devices posed significant challenges, requiring meticulous planning and coordination.

3. Resource Constraints and Time Pressure:

- Limited resources, including skilled personnel, testing tools, and testing environments, strained the testing process and extended project timelines.
- Time pressure from stakeholders and competing project priorities necessitated accelerated testing cycles while maintaining thoroughness and accuracy.

4. Security and Compliance Requirements:

- Stringent security and compliance requirements mandated rigorous testing of security controls, access policies, and data encryption mechanisms.
- Ensuring compliance with industry regulations, data protection laws, and internal security policies added complexity to the testing process and required comprehensive validation.

Strategies for Overcoming Challenges:

1. Comprehensive Testing Planning and Preparation:

- Conducted thorough testing planning and preparation, including inventory assessment, device profiling, and risk analysis, to identify potential challenges and mitigate risks proactively.
- Build the mini version of the testbed covering all the scenarios in production like modern devices and legacy devices to test all the inter operations, etc..
- Developed detailed test plans, scenarios, and methodologies tailored to the specific requirements and constraints of the network migration project.

2. Collaborative Cross-functional Teams:

- Established collaborative cross-functional teams comprising network engineers, security experts, project managers, and stakeholders to facilitate communication, knowledge sharing, and problem-solving.
- Leveraged diverse expertise and perspectives to address complex technical challenges, coordinate testing activities, and align priorities across different departments.

3. Testing Automation and Tooling:

- Leveraged testing automation tools and scripting frameworks to streamline repetitive tasks, automate test execution, and accelerate testing cycles.

- Invested in specialized testing tools for network device emulation, traffic generation, and protocol analysis to simulate real-world scenarios and validate device behavior under varying conditions.

4. Iterative Testing and Validation:

- Adopted an iterative testing approach, conducting incremental testing cycles and validation checkpoints to identify and address issues early in the migration process.
- Implemented phased testing strategies, starting with isolated device testing, followed by integration testing, and culminating in end-to-end validation across the entire network topology.

Outcomes and Lessons Learned:

Successful Migration and Deployment: Most of the challenges were identified at the time of testing in a mini lab setup. Despite the challenges encountered, ABC Enterprises successfully completed the network migration project within the allocated timeframe and budget, minimizing disruption to business operations.

Enhanced Collaboration and Communication: The collaborative efforts of cross-functional teams fostered a culture of teamwork, transparency, and shared accountability, enabling effective problem-solving and decision-making.

Improved Testing Efficiency and Accuracy: Adoption of testing automation tools and methodologies enhanced testing efficiency, reduced manual effort, and improved accuracy, resulting in faster identification and resolution of issues.

Continuous Learning and Improvement: The network migration project served as a learning opportunity, providing valuable insights into testing methodologies, best practices, and areas for improvement in future projects.

Conclusion:

Real-world case studies such as this illustrate the challenges faced and overcome during network device testing in complex migration projects. By leveraging comprehensive planning, collaborative teamwork, innovative tooling, and iterative validation, organizations can navigate testing challenges, achieve successful outcomes, and drive continuous improvement in network performance and reliability. These lessons learned and best practices serve as valuable insights for organizations embarking on similar testing initiatives in the future.

12.3. Lessons Learned

Real-world case studies offer valuable lessons learned from the experiences of organizations navigating network device testing challenges. These lessons provide insights into effective strategies, best practices, and areas for improvement in future testing initiatives. Let's explore a real-world case study highlighting key lessons learned from network device testing.

Case Study: Lessons Learned from a Network Device Testing Project

Organization Background:

A telecommunications company, XYZ Telecom, embarked on a network device testing project to evaluate the performance, reliability, and security of its network infrastructure. The project aimed to identify and address potential vulnerabilities, optimize device configurations, and enhance overall network performance.

Lessons Learned:

1. Thorough Planning and Preparation:

Lesson: Comprehensive planning and preparation are essential for successful testing projects.

XYZ Telecom learned the importance of conducting thorough inventory assessments, device profiling, and risk analysis before initiating testing activities. Clear objectives, well-defined test plans, and alignment with business goals are critical for project success.

2. Collaborative Teamwork and Communication:

Lesson: Collaboration and communication are key to overcoming testing challenges.

The project highlighted the value of collaborative cross-functional teams comprising network engineers, security experts, and project managers. Open communication channels, regular meetings, and knowledge sharing sessions facilitated teamwork, problem-solving, and decision-making.

3. Testing Automation and Tooling:

Lesson: Automation tools enhance testing efficiency and accuracy.

XYZ Telecom recognized the benefits of leveraging testing automation tools and scripting frameworks to streamline testing processes, reduce manual effort, and improve accuracy. Automation enabled faster test execution, enhanced repeatability, and scalability of testing efforts.

4. Iterative Testing and Validation:

Lesson: Iterative testing cycles allow for early identification and resolution of issues.

The project emphasized the importance of conducting iterative testing cycles and validation checkpoints to detect issues early in the testing process. Incremental testing, phased validation, and continuous feedback loops helped prioritize action items and ensure alignment with project objectives.

5. Continuous Learning and Improvement:

Lesson: Continuous learning drives ongoing improvement in testing practices.

XYZ Telecom embraced a culture of continuous learning and improvement, leveraging insights from testing experiences to refine methodologies, enhance processes, and build organizational knowledge. Post-mortem reviews, lessons learned sessions, and knowledge sharing forums facilitated learning and growth.

Conclusion:

The network device testing project undertaken by XYZ Telecom provided valuable lessons learned that can guide future testing initiatives in the organization and beyond. Thorough planning, collaborative teamwork, automation, iterative testing, and continuous improvement are key factors contributing to successful testing outcomes. By embracing these lessons and incorporating them into testing practices, organizations can optimize network performance, enhance security, and drive continuous improvement in their infrastructure. Real-world case studies serve as valuable sources of knowledge and inspiration for organizations embarking on similar testing projects in the future.

Here are some additional areas that can be covered in the "12. Real-world Case Studies:" section:

6. Innovative Solutions and Best Practices:
   - Highlight innovative solutions and best practices implemented during network device testing projects. Showcase creative approaches, unique methodologies, and novel technologies that contributed to successful outcomes.

7. Cost-Benefit Analysis and Return on Investment (ROI):
   - Conduct a cost-benefit analysis and evaluate the ROI of network device testing projects. Assess the financial implications, resource investments, and tangible benefits realized from testing efforts, such as cost savings, productivity gains, and risk mitigation.

8. Customer Testimonials and Endorsements:
   - Include testimonials and endorsements from customers or stakeholders who have benefited from network device testing initiatives. Share real-world experiences, testimonials, and success stories from satisfied clients or internal stakeholders.

9. Industry Benchmarking and Comparative Analysis:
   - Perform industry benchmarking and comparative analysis to assess the performance, security, and reliability of network devices relative to industry standards and peer organizations. Benchmarking data provides valuable insights into competitive positioning and areas for improvement.

10. Regulatory Compliance and Standards Adherence:
    - Explore how network device testing projects ensure compliance with regulatory requirements, industry standards, and best practices. Highlight adherence to standards such as ISO, NIST, GDPR, HIPAA, or PCI DSS, and demonstrate how testing activities support regulatory compliance objectives.

11. Disaster Recovery and Incident Response:
    - Showcase case studies involving disaster recovery and incident response scenarios, where network device testing played a critical role in mitigating risks, minimizing downtime, and facilitating rapid recovery from disruptions or security incidents.

12. Cross-industry Applications and Use Cases:
    ➢ Explore cross-industry applications and use cases of network device testing beyond traditional IT and telecommunications sectors. Highlight how testing methodologies and principles are applied in diverse industries such as healthcare, finance, manufacturing, and transportation.

13. Emerging Technologies and Future Trends:
    ➢ Discuss case studies involving the testing of emerging technologies such as 5G, IoT, SDN, cloud computing, and edge computing. Explore how organizations adapt testing practices to address evolving technological trends and emerging challenges.

14. Sustainability and Green IT Initiatives:
    ➢ Highlight case studies that demonstrate how network device testing contributes to sustainability and green IT initiatives. Showcase energy-efficient configurations, resource optimization strategies, and environmentally responsible practices adopted during testing projects.

These additional areas provide diverse perspectives and insights into the multifaceted aspects of network device testing, showcasing its impact, benefits, and relevance across different industries and contexts. Integrating these topics into the "Real-world Case Studies" section enriches the narrative and provides a holistic view of the challenges, solutions, and outcomes associated with network device testing initiatives.

CHAPTER 13

FUTURE TRENDS IN NETWORK TESTING

13.1. Emerging Technologies in Network Testing

As technology continues to evolve at a rapid pace, the landscape of network testing is also witnessing significant advancements driven by emerging technologies. Understanding these trends is crucial for staying ahead of the curve and leveraging new tools and methodologies to enhance network performance, security, and reliability. Let's explore some of the emerging technologies shaping the future of network testing:

1. Machine Learning and Artificial Intelligence (AI):

   ➤ Machine learning and AI are revolutionizing network testing by enabling intelligent automation, predictive analytics, and anomaly detection. AI-driven algorithms can analyze vast amounts of network data, identify patterns, and predict potential issues before they occur, enhancing proactive network management and troubleshooting.

2. Software-Defined Networking (SDN) and Network Function Virtualization (NFV):

   ➤ SDN and NFV technologies are transforming network architectures by decoupling hardware from software and virtualizing network functions. Network testing in SDN/NFV environments requires new methodologies and tools to validate virtualized network elements, ensure interoperability, and optimize performance in dynamic, software-defined infrastructures.

3. 5G and Edge Computing:

   ➤ The rollout of 5G networks and the proliferation of edge computing are driving the need for specialized network testing solutions tailored to the unique requirements of high-speed, low-latency, and distributed architectures. Network testing in 5G and edge computing environments focuses on validating network slicing, latency-sensitive applications, and edge security mechanisms.

4. Internet of Things (IoT) and Industrial IoT (IIoT):

   ➤ The proliferation of IoT and IIoT devices introduces new challenges for network testing, including device interoperability, scalability, and security. Network testing solutions for IoT environments encompass device profiling, protocol analysis, and performance testing to ensure seamless integration and reliable communication between connected devices.

5. Cloud-native and Containerized Environments:

   ➤ The adoption of cloud-native architectures and containerized applications necessitates new approaches to network testing that align with DevOps principles and continuous integration/continuous deployment (CI/CD) pipelines. Testing methodologies for cloud-native environments focus on container networking, microservices communication, and orchestration platforms such as Kubernetes.

6. Zero Trust Security Frameworks:

   ➤ Zero Trust security frameworks are gaining traction as organizations shift towards a perimeterless security model that assumes no implicit trust within the network. Network testing in Zero Trust environments involves validating access controls, segmentation policies, and identity-based authentication mechanisms to prevent lateral movement and mitigate insider threats.

7. Quantum Computing and Cryptography:

   ➤ The advent of quantum computing poses new challenges and opportunities for network security testing, particularly in the realm of cryptographic algorithms and encryption protocols. Network testing solutions must adapt to quantum-safe cryptography standards and quantum-resistant encryption schemes to protect against future quantum threats.

8. Autonomous Networking and Self-Healing Networks:

   ➤ Autonomous networking technologies leverage AI-driven algorithms to enable self-configuring, self-optimizing, and self-healing networks that adapt dynamically to changing conditions and requirements. Network testing in autonomous networking environments focuses on validating AI-driven decision-making processes, ensuring network resilience, and verifying automated remediation mechanisms.

9. Blockchain for Network Security and Auditing:

   ➤ Blockchain technology holds promise for enhancing network security and auditing capabilities by providing tamper-proof, decentralized ledgers for logging network events, access controls, and configuration changes. Network testing solutions leveraging blockchain enable transparent auditing, immutable record-keeping, and verifiable trust in network transactions and configurations.

10. Open Source Testing Tools and Communities:

    ➤ The proliferation of open source testing tools and communities fosters collaboration, innovation, and knowledge sharing in the field of network testing. Open source projects such as Wireshark, Selenium, and OpenStack contribute to the development of freely available testing frameworks, libraries, and utilities that empower organizations to build customized testing solutions and leverage community-driven expertise.

As organizations embrace these emerging technologies, network testing will evolve to address new challenges and opportunities in the dynamic landscape of modern networking. By staying abreast of these future trends and adopting innovative testing methodologies and tools, organizations can ensure the resilience, security, and performance of their networks in the digital era.

13.2. Evolving Testing Practices

The future of network testing is characterized by the evolution of testing practices to align with emerging technologies, changing network architectures, and evolving business requirements. As organizations embrace digital transformation and adopt innovative networking solutions, testing methodologies must adapt to address new challenges and opportunities. Let's explore some of the evolving testing practices shaping the future of network testing:

1. Shift-Left Testing:
   - Shift-left testing involves moving testing activities earlier in the software development lifecycle (SDLC), enabling early detection and resolution of defects. In the context of network testing, shift-left practices involve integrating testing into the design, planning, and development phases of network infrastructure projects, facilitating proactive validation of configurations, policies, and architectures before deployment.

2. Continuous Testing and Integration:
   - Continuous testing and integration practices promote the seamless integration of testing activities into CI/CD pipelines, enabling rapid feedback loops, automated validation, and continuous improvement. Network testing in CI/CD environments involves automated test execution, integration with version control systems, and real-time monitoring of network changes to ensure the stability, security, and reliability of evolving network infrastructures.

3. DevSecOps and Security Testing:
   - DevSecOps integrates security testing into the DevOps workflow, emphasizing the importance of security throughout the software development lifecycle. In the context of network testing, DevSecOps practices encompass security testing methodologies such as vulnerability scanning, penetration testing, and code analysis to identify and remediate security vulnerabilities early in the development process, enhancing the security posture of network infrastructures.

4. Cloud-based Testing Environments:
   - Cloud-based testing environments leverage cloud infrastructure and services to facilitate scalable, on-demand testing of network configurations, applications, and services. Cloud-based testing platforms provide virtualized testing environments, automated provisioning of resources, and integration with cloud-native tools and technologies, enabling organizations to conduct comprehensive testing in a flexible and cost-effective manner.

5. AI-driven Testing and Automation:
   - AI-driven testing and automation harness the power of artificial intelligence and machine learning algorithms to automate testing tasks, analyze test results, and optimize testing processes. In network testing, AI-driven automation enables intelligent test case generation, predictive analytics, and anomaly detection, accelerating testing cycles, and improving test coverage, accuracy, and efficiency.

6. Context-aware Testing:
   - Context-aware testing considers the unique characteristics and requirements of different network environments, applications, and user scenarios when designing and executing test cases. Context-aware testing methodologies adapt testing strategies, parameters, and success criteria based on contextual factors such as network topology, traffic patterns, and user behavior, ensuring realistic and relevant testing outcomes.

7. Crowdsourced Testing and Bug Bounties:
   - Crowdsourced testing and bug bounty programs leverage the collective intelligence and expertise of external testers and security researchers to identify vulnerabilities and quality issues in network infrastructures. Crowdsourced testing platforms facilitate collaboration, incentivize participation, and provide organizations with access to diverse testing resources and perspectives, enhancing the effectiveness of testing efforts.

8. Quantum-safe Cryptography Testing:
   - With the advent of quantum computing, the need for quantum-safe cryptography testing has emerged to evaluate the resilience of cryptographic algorithms and protocols against quantum attacks. Quantum-safe cryptography testing methodologies assess the security and performance of quantum-resistant encryption schemes and post-quantum cryptographic primitives, ensuring the confidentiality and integrity of network communications in a post-quantum computing era.

9. Compliance-driven Testing Frameworks:
   - Compliance-driven testing frameworks align testing practices with regulatory requirements, industry standards, and organizational policies governing network security, privacy, and data protection. Compliance-driven testing methodologies verify adherence to standards such as GDPR, HIPAA, PCI DSS, and ISO/IEC 27001, providing assurance that network infrastructures meet regulatory and compliance obligations.

10. Self-testing and Self-healing Networks:
    - Self-testing and self-healing networks leverage autonomous networking technologies to enable networks to diagnose, troubleshoot, and remediate issues automatically without human intervention. Self-testing mechanisms continuously monitor network health, detect anomalies, and initiate corrective actions, minimizing downtime, and enhancing network resilience and reliability in dynamic and distributed environments.

By embracing these evolving testing practices, organizations can adapt to the changing demands of modern networking, mitigate risks, and ensure the stability, security, and performance of their network infrastructures in the face of technological advancements and digital transformation initiatives.

13.3. The Role of AI in Network Testing

Artificial Intelligence (AI) is poised to revolutionize the field of network testing, offering advanced capabilities for automation, optimization, and intelligent analysis of network performance, security, and reliability. As AI technologies continue to evolve, their integration into network testing methodologies promises to enhance efficiency, accuracy, and scalability, while addressing the complexities of modern networking environments. Let's explore the role of AI in network testing and its potential impact on the future of testing practices:

1. Automated Test Generation:
   - AI-powered algorithms can automatically generate test cases based on network configurations, traffic patterns, and application requirements. By analyzing network topology and behavior, AI can identify critical test scenarios, prioritize testing efforts, and optimize test coverage, enabling efficient and comprehensive testing of complex network infrastructures.

2. Predictive Analytics and Anomaly Detection:
   - AI-driven predictive analytics algorithms can analyze historical network data to identify patterns, trends, and anomalies indicative of potential issues or performance bottlenecks. By leveraging machine learning models, AI can predict network behavior, anticipate failures, and proactively mitigate risks, enhancing network reliability and resilience.

3. Intelligent Test Orchestration:
   - AI-powered test orchestration platforms can dynamically allocate resources, prioritize test execution, and optimize testing workflows based on real-time network conditions and objectives. By adapting testing strategies to changing environments and requirements, AI enables agile and responsive testing processes that align with business priorities and goals.

4. Natural Language Processing (NLP) for Test Documentation:
   - NLP techniques enable AI systems to analyze and interpret natural language test documentation, requirements, and specifications. By extracting relevant information, identifying dependencies, and generating test scripts or scenarios, AI streamlines the test planning and execution process, reducing manual effort and improving documentation accuracy.

5. Anomaly Detection and Root Cause Analysis:
   - AI-powered anomaly detection algorithms can identify deviations from expected network behavior and pinpoint root causes of performance issues or security threats. By correlating disparate data sources and analyzing network telemetry data in real-time, AI enables rapid incident detection,

diagnosis, and resolution, minimizing downtime and enhancing network troubleshooting capabilities.

6. Virtual Network Simulation and Emulation:

   ➤ AI-driven virtual network simulation and emulation platforms can replicate real-world network environments, applications, and user behavior to facilitate realistic and scalable testing scenarios. By leveraging AI for traffic modeling, scenario generation, and performance prediction, virtual network testing environments enable accurate simulation of complex network interactions and scenarios.

7. Dynamic Test Case Prioritization:

   ➤ AI algorithms can dynamically prioritize test cases based on risk factors, criticality, and impact on business objectives. By analyzing contextual information, historical test results, and feedback from production environments, AI optimizes test execution schedules, resource allocation, and coverage assessment, ensuring efficient use of testing resources and maximizing testing effectiveness.

8. Continuous Learning and Adaptation:

   ➤ AI systems can continuously learn from past testing experiences, feedback, and outcomes to adapt testing strategies, refine models, and improve testing practices over time. By leveraging machine learning algorithms, AI enables adaptive testing methodologies that evolve in response to changing network dynamics, emerging threats, and evolving business requirements.

9. Enhanced Security Testing and Threat Detection:

   ➤ AI-powered security testing tools can analyze network traffic patterns, identify anomalies, and detect potential security threats in real-time. By leveraging machine learning algorithms for pattern recognition, anomaly detection, and behavioral analysis, AI enhances the effectiveness of security testing efforts, enabling proactive threat detection, response, and mitigation.

10. Scalability and Efficiency in Testing:

    ➤ AI-driven automation and optimization techniques improve the scalability and efficiency of network testing processes, enabling organizations to handle large-scale testing initiatives, diverse network environments, and evolving testing requirements. By automating repetitive tasks, optimizing resource utilization, and accelerating test execution, AI enhances the productivity and effectiveness of testing teams.

By harnessing the power of AI technologies, organizations can unlock new capabilities, insights, and efficiencies in network testing, paving the way for more agile, intelligent, and resilient network infrastructures. As AI continues to evolve and mature, its integration into network testing methodologies will drive innovation, enable predictive testing strategies, and empower organizations to meet the challenges of an increasingly complex and dynamic networking landscape.

CHAPTER 14

BEST PRACTICES AND TIPS

14.1. Efficient Test Planning

Efficient test planning is a cornerstone of successful network testing initiatives, ensuring thorough coverage, alignment with business objectives, and optimization of resources. Here are some best practices and tips for efficient test planning in the context of network testing:

1. Define Clear Objectives and Scope:
   - Begin by clearly defining the objectives and scope of the network testing project. Identify the specific goals, requirements, and success criteria for testing, ensuring alignment with business priorities and stakeholder expectations.

2. Understand Network Architecture and Components:
   - Gain a comprehensive understanding of the network architecture, components, and infrastructure under test. Document network topology, configurations, protocols, and dependencies to facilitate accurate test planning and execution.

3. Identify Key Testing Scenarios and Use Cases:
   - Identify and prioritize key testing scenarios and use cases based on critical business functions, user requirements, and potential risks. Consider factors such as performance, security, scalability, and interoperability when selecting testing scenarios.

4. Develop Test Plans and Strategies:
   - Develop detailed test plans and strategies that outline testing objectives, methodologies, timelines, and resource requirements. Define test scenarios, test cases, acceptance criteria, and test data sets to guide testing activities and ensure comprehensive coverage.

5. Collaborate with Cross-functional Teams:
   - Foster collaboration and communication with cross-functional teams, including network engineers, security specialists, system administrators, and business stakeholders. Solicit input from diverse perspectives to identify testing requirements, risks, and constraints.

6. Prioritize Testing Efforts:

   ➤ Prioritize testing efforts based on risk assessment, business impact, and criticality of network components. Focus on testing high-risk areas, critical functionalities, and areas of change to maximize testing effectiveness and efficiency.

7. Allocate Resources and Budget Appropriately:

   ➤ Allocate resources, budget, and personnel appropriately to support testing activities. Ensure sufficient time, manpower, and funding are allocated for planning, execution, and post-testing activities, such as analysis and reporting.

8. Leverage Automation and Tooling:

   ➤ Leverage automation tools, testing frameworks, and scripting languages to streamline testing processes, reduce manual effort, and increase testing efficiency. Automate repetitive tasks, such as test case execution, data generation, and result analysis, to accelerate testing cycles.

9. Perform Risk Analysis and Mitigation:

   ➤ Conduct risk analysis to identify potential threats, vulnerabilities, and dependencies that may impact testing outcomes. Develop risk mitigation strategies and contingency plans to address identified risks and ensure smooth testing operations.

10. Document Test Plans and Results:

    ➤ Document test plans, procedures, and results in a structured and comprehensive manner. Maintain detailed records of testing activities, including test cases, test execution logs, issues encountered, and resolutions implemented, to facilitate traceability and auditability.

11. Iterate and Adapt Testing Strategies:

    ➤ Continuously iterate and adapt testing strategies based on feedback, lessons learned, and evolving network requirements. Embrace an iterative approach to testing, incorporating feedback from stakeholders and real-world experiences to refine testing practices and improve outcomes.

Efficient test planning lays the foundation for successful network testing initiatives, enabling organizations to validate network performance, security, and reliability with confidence. By following these best practices and tips, organizations can optimize testing efforts, minimize risks, and achieve their testing objectives effectively and efficiently.

14.2. Test Execution Strategies

Efficient test execution is essential for validating the performance, security, and reliability of network infrastructures. Here are some best practices and tips for effective test execution in the context of network testing:

1. Follow Test Plans and Procedures:
   - Adhere to the test plans, procedures, and methodologies outlined during the test planning phase. Ensure that testing activities are conducted according to predefined objectives, scenarios, and acceptance criteria to maintain consistency and repeatability.

2. Verify Test Environment Readiness:
   - Verify the readiness of the test environment, including network configurations, hardware resources, and software dependencies, before initiating testing activities. Ensure that all required components are properly configured, accessible, and functioning as expected.

3. Execute Test Cases Systematically:
   - Execute test cases systematically, following a structured approach that covers all planned scenarios and use cases. Prioritize test cases based on risk assessment, criticality, and dependencies, focusing on high-impact areas first to maximize testing effectiveness.

4. Monitor and Measure Test Progress:
   - Monitor and measure test progress regularly to track testing activities, identify bottlenecks, and ensure timely completion of testing milestones. Use test management tools and dashboards to monitor test execution status, identify issues, and communicate progress to stakeholders.

5. Implement Test Automation Wherever Possible:
   - Leverage test automation tools and frameworks to automate repetitive, manual testing tasks, such as test case execution, data validation, and result verification. Automate regression tests, performance tests, and routine maintenance tasks to increase testing efficiency and reliability.

6. Conduct Parallel and Distributed Testing:
   - Conduct parallel and distributed testing to accelerate test execution and improve resource utilization. Distribute test cases across multiple test environments, devices, or network segments to reduce testing time and increase test coverage while maintaining consistency and reliability.

7. Emulate Real-world Scenarios and Traffic Patterns:
   - Emulate real-world network scenarios and traffic patterns during test execution to simulate actual usage conditions and identify potential performance bottlenecks or security vulnerabilities. Use traffic generation tools, network emulators, and load generators to generate realistic test traffic and measure system response under varying loads.

8. Monitor System Health and Performance:
   - Monitor system health and performance metrics during test execution to identify anomalies, bottlenecks, and deviations from expected behavior. Use network monitoring tools, performance monitoring dashboards, and logging mechanisms to capture real-time data and troubleshoot issues promptly.

9. Validate Results and Verify Compliance:
   - Validate test results against expected outcomes and acceptance criteria defined in the test plan. Verify compliance with regulatory requirements, industry standards, and organizational policies governing network performance, security, and reliability.

10. Document Test Execution and Report Findings:
    - Document test execution activities, including test case execution logs, test results, issues encountered, and resolutions implemented. Prepare comprehensive test reports summarizing key findings, observations, and recommendations for stakeholders' review and decision-making.

11. Iterate and Refine Test Execution Processes:
    - Continuously iterate and refine test execution processes based on feedback, lessons learned, and evolving testing requirements. Embrace a culture of continuous improvement, incorporating insights from previous testing cycles to optimize test execution strategies and enhance testing outcomes.

By following these best practices and tips, organizations can streamline test execution processes, improve testing efficiency, and ensure the accuracy, reliability, and effectiveness of network testing initiatives. Effective test execution is essential for validating network performance, security, and reliability, enabling organizations to maintain robust and resilient network infrastructures in today's dynamic and interconnected world.

14.3. Continuous Improvement in Testing Processes

Continuous improvement is essential for ensuring the effectiveness, efficiency, and relevance of network testing processes over time. Here are some best practices and tips for fostering continuous improvement in network testing:

1. Establish a Culture of Learning and Innovation:
   - Foster a culture of learning, innovation, and continuous improvement within the testing team and across the organization. Encourage collaboration, knowledge sharing, and experimentation to identify new techniques, tools, and methodologies for enhancing network testing practices.

2. Collect and Analyze Feedback:
   - Solicit feedback from stakeholders, testers, and end-users to gather insights into the strengths, weaknesses, and opportunities for improvement in network testing processes. Analyze feedback systematically, identify recurring themes or trends, and prioritize areas for enhancement.

3. Conduct Post-Mortem Reviews:
   - Conduct post-mortem reviews or retrospective sessions at the conclusion of testing cycles to reflect on successes, challenges, and lessons learned. Identify root causes of issues, discuss potential

improvements, and develop action plans for addressing gaps and opportunities identified during testing.

4. Embrace Continuous Integration and Deployment (CI/CD):

   ➤ Embrace CI/CD practices to automate the integration, testing, and deployment of network configurations, applications, and services. Implement automated testing pipelines, version control systems, and continuous monitoring tools to streamline testing processes and accelerate delivery cycles.

5. Leverage Metrics and KPIs:

   ➤ Define and track key performance indicators (KPIs) and metrics to measure the effectiveness, efficiency, and quality of network testing efforts. Monitor metrics such as test coverage, defect density, test cycle time, and mean time to resolution (MTTR) to assess progress and identify areas for improvement.

6. Implement Agile Testing Methodologies:

   ➤ Adopt agile testing methodologies, such as Scrum or Kanban, to promote iterative, incremental testing practices that align with the pace of software development and deployment. Break down testing tasks into smaller, manageable units, prioritize testing activities, and adapt testing plans based on evolving requirements and feedback.

7. Invest in Training and Skill Development:

   ➤ Invest in training and skill development programs to enhance the competencies and capabilities of testing teams. Provide opportunities for testers to acquire new technical skills, domain knowledge, and certifications relevant to network testing, cybersecurity, automation, and emerging technologies.

8. Encourage Experimentation and Innovation:

   ➤ Encourage testers to experiment with new tools, techniques, and approaches for network testing. Create a safe environment for innovation and experimentation, where testers can explore alternative solutions, prototype new methodologies, and challenge conventional wisdom to drive continuous improvement.

9. Establish Communities of Practice:

   ➤ Establish communities of practice or knowledge-sharing forums where testers can collaborate, exchange ideas, and share best practices related to network testing. Encourage participation in professional associations, online forums, and industry events to stay informed about emerging trends and practices in network testing.

10. Regularly Review and Update Testing Processes:

    ➤ Regularly review and update testing processes, methodologies, and standards to reflect evolving business needs, technology trends, and industry best practices. Conduct periodic audits or assessments of testing processes to identify areas for optimization and refinement.

11. Celebrate Achievements and Recognize Contributions:

   ▶ Celebrate achievements and recognize contributions made by testing teams to promote a culture of appreciation and motivation. Acknowledge individual and team successes, milestones, and innovations in network testing, reinforcing the importance of continuous improvement and excellence.

By implementing these best practices and tips, organizations can cultivate a culture of continuous improvement in network testing, driving innovation, efficiency, and quality in testing processes. Continuous improvement enables organizations to adapt to changing requirements, overcome challenges, and deliver reliable, high-quality network solutions that meet the needs of stakeholders and end-users.

CHAPTER 15

CONCLUSION

15.1. Summary of Key Takeaways

Throughout this comprehensive guide to network testing, we've explored various aspects of planning, executing, and optimizing testing processes to ensure the reliability, performance, and security of network infrastructures. Here are the key takeaways from each topic covered:

1. Introduction to Network Testing:
   - Network testing is critical in ensuring the functionality, performance, and security of network infrastructures.
   - The landscape of network testing is evolving rapidly, driven by technological advancements and changing business requirements.

2. Fundamentals of Network Testing:
   - Understanding networks, protocols, and communication basics is essential for effective network testing.
   - Different types of networks, including LAN, WAN, and MAN, require tailored testing approaches to address their unique characteristics and challenges.

3. Types of Network Testing:
   - Functional testing verifies network services, connectivity, and data integrity.
   - Performance testing assesses bandwidth, latency, scalability, and throughput.
   - Security testing identifies vulnerabilities, conducts penetration tests, and evaluates firewall and IDS systems.
   - Compatibility testing ensures device and platform interoperability and browser compatibility.
   - Stress testing evaluates network resilience under overload, resource exhaustion, and failover scenarios.

4. Test Planning and Strategy:
   - Defining clear objectives, scope, and key components is crucial for effective test planning.

- Developing test cases, scenarios, and strategies helps ensure comprehensive coverage and alignment with business goals.

5. Test Tools and Technologies:
- A wide range of testing tools and frameworks are available for network testing, including both industry-standard and proprietary solutions.
- Automation, virtualization, and emulation technologies enhance testing efficiency and scalability.

6. Functional Testing:
- Functional testing validates network services, connectivity, and data integrity, utilizing testbed topologies and packet flow analysis for in-depth verification.

7. Performance Testing:
- Performance testing evaluates bandwidth, latency, scalability, and throughput to assess network performance under varying conditions.

8. Security Testing:
- Security testing identifies vulnerabilities, conducts penetration tests, and evaluates firewall and IDS systems to ensure network security.

9. Compatibility Testing:
- Compatibility testing ensures device and platform interoperability, browser compatibility, and compliance with industry standards.

10. Stress Testing:
- Stress testing evaluates network resilience under overload, resource exhaustion, and failover scenarios to identify potential weaknesses and bottlenecks.

11. Reporting and Documentation:
- Comprehensive reporting and documentation are essential for communicating test results, findings, and recommendations to stakeholders effectively.

12. Real-world Case Studies:
- Real-world case studies provide insights into successful implementations, challenges faced, lessons learned, and best practices in network testing.

13. Future Trends in Network Testing:
- Emerging technologies such as AI, automation, and virtualization will play a significant role in shaping the future of network testing, enabling more intelligent, efficient, and scalable testing practices.

14. Best Practices and Tips:
- Efficient test planning, execution, and continuous improvement are essential for achieving successful outcomes in network testing.

In conclusion, network testing is a dynamic and multifaceted discipline that requires careful planning, execution, and ongoing refinement to ensure the reliability, performance, and security of network infrastructures. By following best practices, leveraging advanced technologies, and embracing continuous improvement, organizations can optimize their testing efforts and build robust and resilient networks capable of meeting the demands of today's digital landscape.

15.2. Encouragement for Continuous Learning

As we conclude this comprehensive guide to network testing, it's essential to emphasize the value of continuous learning and professional development in the field of IT and network testing. In the ever-evolving landscape of technology, staying abreast of the latest trends, tools, and methodologies is paramount to remain competitive and effective in your role as an IT professional. Here's why continuous learning is crucial:

1. **Rapid Technological Advancements:** Technology is advancing at an unprecedented pace, with new tools, frameworks, and techniques emerging regularly. By staying curious and proactive in learning about these advancements, you can leverage the latest innovations to enhance your network testing capabilities.

2. **Complexity of Networking Environments:** Modern networking environments are becoming increasingly complex, with diverse infrastructures, protocols, and applications. Continuous learning enables you to understand and navigate this complexity effectively, ensuring that you can address the diverse challenges of network testing with confidence.

3. **Adaptation to Changing Requirements:** Business requirements and user expectations are constantly evolving, necessitating flexibility and adaptability in network testing approaches. By embracing continuous learning, you can acquire new skills and knowledge to adapt your testing strategies to meet changing demands effectively.

4. **Optimization of Testing Practices:** Continuous learning empowers you to optimize your testing practices and methodologies based on industry best practices, lessons learned, and emerging trends. By regularly evaluating and refining your testing processes, you can drive efficiencies, improve outcomes, and deliver greater value to your organization.

5. **Professional Growth and Career Advancement:** Investing in continuous learning not only enhances your technical skills but also contributes to your professional growth and career advancement. By expanding your knowledge and expertise in network testing, you position yourself as a valuable asset to your organization and open up opportunities for advancement in your career.

To support your journey of continuous learning in network testing, consider the following actions:

Stay Curious: Remain curious and eager to explore new ideas, technologies, and methodologies related to network testing. Take initiative to research and learn about emerging trends, tools, and best practices in the field.

Seek Training and Certification: Pursue training programs, workshops, and certifications that align with your interests and career goals in network testing. Invest in formal education and professional development opportunities to deepen your expertise and credentials in the field.

Engage with Communities: Engage with online forums, user groups, and professional associations dedicated to network testing and IT. Participate in discussions, share insights, and learn from the experiences of peers and industry experts in the community.

Experiment and Practice: Experiment with different tools, techniques, and scenarios in your testing environment to gain hands-on experience and practical skills. Set up lab environments, conduct experiments, and apply theoretical knowledge to real-world testing challenges.

Stay Updated: Regularly monitor industry news, blogs, and publications to stay updated on the latest developments in network testing and IT. Follow thought leaders, subscribe to relevant newsletters, and attend conferences or webinars to stay informed about emerging trends and innovations.

By embracing a mindset of continuous learning and professional growth, you can unlock new opportunities, expand your capabilities, and make meaningful contributions to the field of network testing and IT. Remember that learning is a lifelong journey, and each new skill or piece of knowledge you acquire brings you one step closer to achieving your goals and realizing your full potential as an IT professional.

APPENDIX

Glossary of Terms:

1. **Network Testing:** The process of evaluating the performance, reliability, and security of network infrastructures through various testing techniques and methodologies.
2. **LAN (Local Area Network):** A network that connects computers and devices within a limited geographical area, such as a home, office, or campus.
3. **WAN (Wide Area Network):** A network that spans a large geographical area and connects multiple LANs or other networks.
4. **MAN (Metropolitan Area Network):** A network that covers a larger geographical area than a LAN but smaller than a WAN, typically serving a city or metropolitan area.
5. **Protocol:** A set of rules and conventions governing the format and transmission of data between devices on a network.
6. **Functional Testing:** Testing that verifies the functionality and behavior of network components, services, and applications.
7. **Performance Testing:** Testing that assesses the performance and scalability of network infrastructures, including bandwidth, latency, and throughput.
8. **Security Testing:** Testing that identifies vulnerabilities, threats, and risks in network systems and evaluates measures to mitigate them.
9. **Compatibility Testing:** Testing that ensures the compatibility and interoperability of network devices, platforms, and applications.
10. **Stress Testing:** Testing that evaluates the resilience and stability of network systems under extreme conditions, such as high traffic loads or resource exhaustion.

Additional Resources:

1. Books:

"Network Security Testing" by Chris McMahon

2. Online Courses:

Coursera: "Networking in Google Cloud: Hybrid Connectivity and Network Management"

Udemy: "Network Penetration Testing by using Python"

Pluralsight: "Advanced Network Troubleshooting"

3. Websites and Blogs:

Networking Academy: Cisco's online platform for networking education and resources.

PacketLife: A blog and community dedicated to networking topics, including testing and troubleshooting.

Network Computing: A website offering articles, webinars, and resources on network testing and optimization.

4. Tools and Software:

Wireshark: A widely-used network protocol analyzer for capturing and analyzing network traffic.

Nmap: A powerful network scanning tool for discovering hosts and services on a network.

Selenium: An automation tool commonly used for web application testing, including network-related functionalities.

JUnit: Programmers-friendly testing framework for Java and the JVM

Robot Framework: https://robotframework.org

JUnit 5: https://junit.org

pytest: https://pytest.org

References and Citations:

Clyde F. Coombs, Jr. Catherine A. Coombs

Communications Network Test & Measurement Handbook. 1998 The McGraw-Hill Companies, Inc.

McMahon, Chris. Network Security Assessment, 3rd Edition. O'Reilly Media, Inc., 2016.

This appendix provides a glossary of key terms, additional resources for further learning, and references to books, courses, websites, and tools relevant to network testing. These resources can serve as valuable supplements to the information presented in this guide, helping readers deepen their understanding and expertise in network testing.

Milton Keynes UK
Ingram Content Group UK Ltd.
UKHW051340011224
451734UK00006B/102